Castlemorton Farmer
John Rayer Lane 1798 - 1871

Castlemorton Farmer
John Rayer Lane 1798 - 1871

Pamela Hurle

Illustrated by
Charles Grant

Published by
Pamela Hurle, Storridge,
Malvern, Worcestershire

© Text — Pamela Hurle, 1996
© Illustrations — Charles Grant, 1996

ISBN 0 9529366 0 7

Typeset and Printed by
Record Printers,
Bromyard, Herefordshire.

Contents

List of Illustrations
Introduction and Acknowledgements

	Page
Chapter One 1822-1823 An Earnest Young Man	1
Chapter Two 1845-1848 The Respected Farmer	17
Chapter Three 1850-1852 A Man of the World	27
Chapter Four 1854-1856 The Prime of Life	37
Chapter Five 1857-1859 A Pillar of the Community	47
Chapter Six 1864-1871 Human Frailties	55
Epilogue	64

List of Illustrations

	Page
Hurst Farm	1
Barn at Hurst Farm	2
Hill Court Farm	3
Moor Court	3
Hanley Hall	4
Blackmore Park Farm	4
Welland Court	5
Hillend Court	9
Old Church of St. James, Welland	11
Cutlers Farm	15
Bronsil	18
Bottom of Quay Lane, Hanley Castle	22
Somers Arms Hotel, Eastnor	41
The Pheasant at Welland	45
The Feathers Inn, Castlemorton	49
St. Gregory's Church, Castlemorton	58
The Robin Hood, Castlemorton	61
Map	65
Pages from John Rayer Lane's diaries	26, 32 & 33

Introduction and Acknowledgements

In medieval times Castlemorton lay deep in the forest known as Malvern Chase. Even now, in its open common and scrubland and in the shadow of its trees and lanes, it is possible to sense something of the atmosphere of that great hunting ground.

John Rayer Lane, who was born in the late 18th century, spent his whole life in Castlemorton, leaving a remarkable legacy, hitherto known only to a few people: the diaries, which he called "Memorandums", kept regularly throughout his life. It is most generous of his namesake and other members of his family to permit me to use his work as the basis for this publication. Particular thanks are due to the Rev. Canon Ruth Wintle who, by alerting Miss Veronica Owen, churchwarden of Castlemorton, to the existence of these diaries, enabled me to locate them after many years of fruitless search.

Sadly some volumes have been lost without trace, but those which remain are more than enough to provide a colourful picture of 19th century rural life as seen through the eyes of an articulate fairly well-to-do farmer. Regrettable though it is that some are missing, the surviving diaries cover vital periods of change and development - 1822-3, 1845-8, 1850-52, 1854-9 and 1864-71. They are a rich legacy indeed.

Many entries are of day-to-day duties: sowing the seed, reaping the harvest, selling produce from the land, the sheep and the cattle. Analysis of these regular activities of the farming year simply reinforces much which is common knowledge; publication of such minutiae alone would not be very interesting or worthwhile. What make John Rayer Lane's diary worthy of publication are the breadth of his knowledge and his often pithy comment on both local and national affairs. Highlights in his life were his occasional visits to Birmingham, London or Kent - places about which few locals knew anything: indeed, his own wife seems not to have ventured further than Malvern, Worcester and her home parish of Pendock. She figured surprisingly little in his diary and when he referred to her it was as "Mrs. Lane" or "Mrs. L."

Lane's account is of much more than local interest: he commented on national events such as the Great Exhibition of 1851 (which he visited), the Crimean War (in which he was conscious of the human cost) and the political difficulties of successive governments led by men such as Peel, Palmerston and Disraeli. Through it all runs the tragi-comedy of human nature, constant target of his dry wit.

Though his spelling was that of a well-educated man, his punctuation was often shaky, making his meaning ambiguous to the modern reader - for which we can scarcely blame him since he believed himself to be writing a personal record solely for his own use. I have occasionally felt it necessary to insert commas, full-stops or capital letters in order to make sense of the writing, but have otherwise quoted verbatim from his original version which so spontaneously reflects his wit and apparently unconscious humour.

While working on this text I met some delightfully helpful members of the Lane family, including his 101 year old great grand-daughter, Vera Wintle, and her daughter, Ruth. It was also a pleasure to find such interest in my project from Christina and Jeffrey Leake who now farm part of the land once farmed by John Rayer Lane and live in his former home, Cutlers Farm.

I most fortunately, too, met Charles Grant, whose evocative drawings have so much enhanced this publication. It has been a joy to work with such an enthusiast and I am extremely grateful for his ready help.

A child of wartime London, I was introduced to the countryside by the farmer's son who became my husband. I thank him for teaching this Londoner to love the countryside and for giving me the understanding that so much increases my appreciation of John Rayer Lane and his world.

Pamela Hurle
August 1996

Chapter One 1822 - 1823
An Earnest Young Man

John Rayer Lane, second son of William and Elizabeth Lane, was born on 16th May 1798 in Castlemorton, probably at the Hurst Farm which his father farmed until he died in 1817. William's 45 year old widow, Elizabeth, was left with their six children, the youngest a five year old daughter, but maintained a comfortable life-style until her death in 1863 at the age of 90.

HURST FARM

Her sons William and Alfred seem to have stayed with her at the Hurst, but at Candlemas (February) 1824 John Rayer Lane, aged 25, took over neighbouring Cutlers Farm and was to farm it until he died in 1871.

His first surviving diary covers the period January 1822 to December 1823 and reveals quite a self-possessed young man. The opening entry on 1st January 1822 shows that in his early twenties he had the gravitas of many a landowner twice his age:

1

> "I can never remember a year begin under more unfavorable (sic) auspices as regarding agriculture, the last year's crop being so much injured by the wet weather is now selling as follows: Wheat from 2/6 to 6/-; Beans 3/- to 3/6; Barley 2/- to 3/6... As to this year's crop, tis about one half sown in this neighbourhood and in some places scarce any, the land still in a very wet and awkward condition. As to live stock the sale is quite as bad as grain, Beef 3½d to 4d.... In short the graziers find a very great difficulty in obtaining the same prices for their fat cows and sheep as they gave for them last spring. In general rents are as high as ever, and tithes, parochial and other taxes are reduced but very little. In brief Farmers never knew the times so bad before but it cannot much longer continue in this state and may Providence soon alter it is the prayer of us all.
> Thus having given an outline of the state of things at the present time I shall briefly mention the principal transactions of Myself thro the Year for my own perusal, hoping never to see any circumstance recorded in this book at which I shall have reason to repent....J.R.L."

OLD BARN AT HURST FARM

Such solemn commentary might lead one to suppose he was a very sober young man, but his entries for several following weeks clearly show that in fact he enjoyed life immensely, attending parties till all hours in the morning at the larger local houses:

> "January 1822
> 1st   Dined with a party and spent the evening at the Moor Court till 2 o'clock.
> 2nd   Spent the evening and night at Hillend Court with the singers very merrily till 7 next morning.

3rd Dined at my Grandmother's. Spent the evening merry till 3
6th Spent the evening at Hillend
7th Spent the evening at Greenfields with a party of Uptonians till 3
8th Spent the evening at Hill Court with a party very merrily till 4 o'clock

HILL COURT FARM

9th Spent the evening at Mr. Clews with a party... till 2 o'clock
10th Went to Upton New Market. Spent the evening at the Crown.
11th Mr and Mrs Hill and Sturkey spent the evening at the Hurst till 2 o'clock
12th Went to Worcester New Market. Dined and drank wine at the Bell
13th Spent a pleasant evening at the Moor Court. E.C.xx"

.... and so it went on!

MOOR COURT

This entry for 13th January contains his first coy reference to Elizabeth Clarke, whose family home was Moor Court. She was to become his wife, and early diary entries are peppered with her initials, often followed by some little kisses (xx).

As we have seen, he had social confidence as a regular visitor to the homes of long-established middle-class families in Castlemorton and neighbouring parishes, such as Hanley Hall or Blackmore Park.

HANLEY HALL

At Welland Court he sometimes "smoked a pipe or two" with Mr. Twinberrow. On Good Friday 1822 he went again to Welland, accompanying the singers at the little church next to Welland Court and spending the evening "in a musical way" next door with the vicar, the Rev. William Boulter. The church was demolished and replaced in 1873-5 by the present church at Welland cross-roads, but the delightful old vicarage remains, as does the refurbished Court.

BLACKMORE PARK FARM

WELLAND COURT

Between his jottings about his social life we find references to the serious work of the year: 25th February saw the beginning of bean planting, finished on 15th March. Barley sowing was finished on 3rd May and haymaking on 9th July. On 15th May, one of a party of 15 gentlemen, he killed 8 birds at the rook shooting, an occasion when work was mixed with pleasure.

The mix of business with pleasure was, as for so many farmers, his life-blood. Sales - of produce, stock or property - attracted crowds then as now; John Rayer Lane loved them, developing a shrewd eye from a young age. Low prices were reflected in his comments on both Worcester Market on 19th January and Ledbury Fair on 4th February - "very dull" - while Worcester Market on 23rd February was "the dullest I ever did see." A cow fetched £51 and a bull £41 at Mr. Price's four day sale of "capital stock" at Little Malvern at the end of February. The Pheasant Inn at Welland was up for sale on 20th May but did not sell. Although Worcester Fair on 30th March was "very dull" he stopped to see Mr Ingleby the conjuror perform and with his companion got "fresh", his usual adjective to describe himself after over-indulgence in drink.

Sometimes greater excitements occurred, as when he attended "Meredith's trial" at the Worcester sessions and went on to spend the evening with a Glee Club at the Reindeer - "very capital singing". The crime and the fate of Meredith are not clear but the vitality of the inn which gave its name to one of modern Worcester's pedestrianised shopping areas is obvious.

In later life John Rayer Lane recorded little interest in clothes, except to note the occasional purchase of a new coat or pair of shoes - especially if they hurt. But in his younger days, like most young men, he liked to cut a dash in new clothes. On 21st April he "put on a pair of new boots" and on 31st May he "put on a New

Blue Coat" for an exciting coach journey to Birmingham, then a new town bustling with activity brought about by the industrial revolution of the 18th century. He saw much that he had never seen or even imagined in his life. With a Mr. Chantry he went to a fair attended by "the most people I ever saw together." On 1st June he went with Mr. Chantry to his Birmingham "manufactory of paper Japan wares", the smell of which he did not like. The Eagle foundry was "the largest iron warehouse I ever saw." He approved of the new church of St. Philip, going to the top of it for "a very fine view of Birmingham." The day was rounded off by watching "Tom and Jerry or Life in London" in the "hansomest theatre I ever saw."

The next morning he "went to drink Leamington water but did not like it." Then he visited the "Jews Burying Ground but could not read the gravestones, being in Hebrew." His activities on this Sunday point to the flourishing state of religion in the 1820s and were themselves surprisingly ecumenical: he went to the Roman Catholic chapel with its "hansome alter and crucifix" in front of which worshippers were at "their silent devotions" and then on to the equally "hansome" Free Church with its "mahogany seats, fine toned organ" and "congregational singing." In the afternoon he visited the ancient and spacious church of St. Martin where it was "a grand sight to see the congregation from the organ loft." St. Paul's, too, was "very hansome indeed" but St. Mary's Chapel was disappointing, being shut up. Carr's Lane Calvinist Chapel was a very elegant modern building but the singing was indifferent. He went to evening service in another Calvinist chapel - Ebenezer. It was "a truly elegant place" with mahogany seats "and a very beautiful chandelier lighted with gas." This modern scientific marvel enabled him to see that "there were full 2000 present. I did not like the doctrine but was strongly invited to go again." In short, "all the places of worship were well filled but the greater part of the population of Birmingham seem to be Dissenters of one sect or other." Clearly this loyal member of the established church from rural Worcestershire was not to be seduced by the religious fervour of the nonconformists. He showed, however, throughout this comprehensive sampling of religious practices a mind much more open than it became in his later years.

After Sunday's extraordinary diet of religious services he next concentrated on some of Birmingham's flourishing industries. On the morning of Monday 3rd June he was off to Chantry's pocket book manufactory where every day 10 men each made 8 dozen pocket books. Mr. Walton, a jeweller, employed 30 or 40 men "in the goldsmithing." Another 30 men were employed at Mr. Potts' brass foundry - "a very curious process."

Unlike these hard-pressed generators of Birmingham's prosperity, in the afternoon he was able to go with a friend to Vauxhall Gardens - "the finest pleasure ground I ever saw" - and thence to the Barracks, "a very extensive yard surrounded by stabling and centinels always parading." Next he went to the "Glass Manufactory, very curious but almost insufferable hot."

On 4th June he was handsomely treated at a dinner where two ladies played "uncommonly well on the pianoforte". There were more visits to churches, as well as to Aston Hall, "a very ancient and truly beautiful seat" set in Aston Park with the "longest brick wall I ever saw." He recounted the familiar tale that it was here that "King Charles was concealed and there is a round hole in the staircase made by a cannon ball at that time, the ball to be seen even now." At the Aston Tavern he saw the "very pleasant tea garden and a prettyish girl" and "spent the pleasantest evening since being at Birmingham" with a few friends before finding himself locked out of his lodgings!

In truth, he was a country lad, for whom the charms of town life soon palled. By 5th June he had had enough, bluntly summarising his experiences of the last few days:

> *"Being quite tired of Birmingham I determined to return home, the weather being so very hot and the rank smell of the town made me quite unwell - before I leave this subject 'tis but justice to say that I never met with more hospitality than at Birmingham. They are ingenious and good natured, short and swarthy complexion and very few hansome women or men."*

Back home the usual social round continued. During the summer months variety was added to the evenings spent at the homes of friends because it was the season for wakes - the forerunners of today's church fetes. Originally held to commemorate the founding of a church, wakes were a curious combination of religious observance and rumbustious merrymaking.

On 24th June he went with John Spencer to Mathon Wake, staying all night. He "went to see Miss Woodyatt on the morrow - she's strangly alter'd." Tantalisingly, we are not told in what way. He was honest enough to admit to spending 26th June "in an idle way with Mr. W. Smith" at Mathon and he "had a scuffle with a scotchman at Ravenhills." On 30th there was another wake at Morton Green.

On 17th July he stayed at the Pheasant in Welland until midnight, then went to the Rhydd before walking home to the Hurst. This sounds like quite an exhausting evening - especially in the absence of today's ubiquitous street lights and electric torches. He admitted that he "drank to freely of Wm. Harris's cyder" on 25th. Welland Wake followed on 28th July and 2 days later he "had a spree at Harris's with Mister Barron Baylis alias Smith and Neate." .

Between all the frivolity the real business of the countryside had to go on. His haymaking was finished on 9th July "being the shortest haymaking and the least hay ever remembered" and on 29th July he was presumably sober enough when he went with Mr. Hill and John Rayer to impound "all stock that did not belong to occupiers of land in the Meadows." It was a serious matter for animals to graze on land to which their owners had no entitlement, especially in a season when hay was in short supply.

Occasional misfortunes are recorded. On 10th June Mr and Mrs. Hill of Hillend Court were thrown out of their gig near the Hurst Farm and on 14th July his own grandmother, who must have been about 70 years old, was thrown off her horse "and hurt very badly." A different kind of unpleasantness occurred on 23rd when he "discharged Betty Turner without any wages for abuse and neglect of work."

Mostly, however, life was very pleasant. The evening of August 4th was spent at Mr. Sturkey's with George Boulter and Capt. Barratt "who got famously drunk." On 6th he went to Worcester with "the team" (presumably horses) to take beans to Nicholls, and the next day the "halling" (hauling) of 17 loads of wheat was finished earlier than he ever remembered. The day ended with supper at the home of William Harris, where they had a shoulder of venison and he got "very fresh", drinking gin. Having sobered up, he guiltily noted: "N.B. Will do so no more."

On 14th August the running at Worcester races was "pretty good". After the races he went to the theatre to see "The Heir at Law" and a farce "spoil'd child" with his cousin, John Rayer. His uncle William Rayer was very ill so our hero called on him on 19th and then smoked a pipe at Hillend with Mr. Lord and another friend. Pipe-smoking, a virility symbol drawing together different generations, was an important social activity: more pipes were smoked at Sturkeys with Capt. Barratt and W. Harris on 20th.

HILLEND COURT

His entry for 23rd August is rather a mystery. It reads "Apeal Day at Upton got off the duty of an house dog 8/-." Upton at that time was a bustling market town, much more important than Malvern, and it was possible to watch plays at the theatre there. On 29th August he saw the "tragedy of Geo. Barnwell at Upton." His friend, D. Davies, was made "very tipsy afterwards." Hopefully everyone behaved better next week at "a Dance with some girls at Mr. Tombs." Captain Barratt was "very ill" on the 13th and, given his fondness for liquor, one draws the obvious conclusion. On 17th September John Rayer Lane went with a friend and Miss Lloyd, the "favourite" at a dance the previous evening, to Malvern Wells where he spent a pleasant day though, somewhat enigmatically, he observed that "Mr. Clarke come and was very uneasy." 20th September was "a pleasant day" at Bushley with Miss Lloyd whom he described as "a very pleasant girl." The evenings of the 22nd and 23rd were also enjoyably spent with Miss Lloyd but the next day she "returned home in a gig with Mr. J. Clarke of Ashelworth" - apparently the second time that Mr. Clarke had cast a cloud over proceedings. During this period the presence of both Miss Lloyd and Miss Elizabeth Clarke is noted at numerous social functions, and perhaps he was unable to decide whom he preferred. Eventually the matter seems to have been decided for him: next year, on 5th May 1823, Miss Lloyd married Mr. Clarke. "I wish them luck" was his laconic observation on what was possibly a personal disappointment. It took another 2½ years for him to marry Elizabeth Clarke on 30th November 1825, when he was 27½ and she was nearly 39.

Business deals featured as importantly as his social life. In late August he sold all the fruit of Browlows Orchard for £2.10.0. A week later Mr. Price's "things sold very cheap" at a sale at Malvern Wood. Dissatisfied with the "bad price" he obtained on 19th September at Worcester fair for 11 fat sheep - 15/6d each - he was better pleased with his sale next week at Upton of "11 strong pigs". On the way to Worcester market, where he sold 80 bushels of barley on 21st September, he struck up conversation in the horse-drawn coach from Malvern to Worcester "with the celebrated Mr. Lindley who recommended some music for the violincello."

October 1822 was full of interest. On the 5th he "went a hunting with the Collwall Hounds round Castlemorton - pretty good sport." Next day he went to Worcester market and drank tea with the very pleasant Miss Lloyd. Two days later he went to a play in Upton with Miss Clarke and then on to Greenfields with her. The play coincided with his visit to Upton Mop, the regular hiring fair held in market towns such as Upton. These were major events in the farming year, when labourers and skilled men sought employment and farmers would pick the likeliest looking workers for their farms. These colourful outdoor events at which workers carried items such as shepherds' crooks as symbolic tokens of their trades, were the noisy precursors of today's bleak and uncomfortable job-centres. The mop lasted for several days: perhaps local preoccupation with the mop accounted for the "uncommonly low " prices fetched at a sale at Hillend on the 9th. Possibly, too, it was at this mop that he found the man whom he hired for £4 on 11th October. A few days later he noted a visit "to Great Malvern to enquire the character of a servant for Mr. Rayer." A personal call on a previous employer was the very sensible, but more time-consuming, equivalent of today's telephone enquiry as to the suitability of a new employee.

John Rayer Lane had close connections with the Rayers and on 20th October, a very wet day, "smoked a pipe with J. Rayer instead of going to church." Perhaps he was compensating for this on 10th November when he "dined at Hill Court and spent the evening singing psalms etc with Mr. Rayer."

At the end of October he attended an inquest on a poor man who hanged himself; a couple of days later he saw Richard Cross and his bride Sarah Hart. His cryptic "quite a *cold* wedding" was not, presumably, a reference to the temperature in the church. Some entries are especially puzzling: for example, on 9th November he "bought a case of Instruments" for 15 shillings, but never referred to them again - not even to specify what they were for. They may have been veterinary tools for dealing with minor ailments of the farm stock but perhaps they were musical: on 25th, after attending an "Inquest at the Pheasant on an old woman found drown'd in Dainmoor Brook", he spent another musical evening at Rev. William Boulter's vicarage by Welland old church.

THE OLD CHURCH OF ST JAMES WELLAND

As a young farmer, he noted the audit days when farming dues and tithes had to be paid to landowners and to the church. Once the necessary business had been done - often at an inn - the assembled crowd would talk and entertain themselves, doubtless well oiled by freely flowing food and drink. On 21st November, for example, the audit at Eastnor Farm was followed by "a jovial evening although times are bad." About the same time he "finished drink making", having made countless hogheads of it and "sold 300 kipes of fruit" - presumably cider apples. (A kipe was a round basket holding about 2½ pecks dry measure or 5 gallons). Next day "Mr. W. Harris and J Spencer got very drunk at Mr. Clews's. I took Spencer home afterwards." A tithe audit on 5th was the "windiest night I ever remember" and no drunkenness was recorded.

Christmas, like New Year, was always a time for family parties and John Rayer Lane fittingly concluded 1822 with the comment that it was "a year in which I have very much enjoy'd myself. May the next ensuing be as Happy." He had

11

just acquired a new toy: on 30th December he had "fired the double-barrelled gun the first time." It cost him five guineas and came from his Birmingham friend, Mr. Chantry, who came to stay for a few days at the beginning of 1823 when the party season was in full swing. The exact meaning of "Took Arthur Clarke's girl Miss Wood off him" is not clear but was significant enough to have been noted! On 18th January he "Sat down and smoked for 12 hours at home with J Spencer and J Clews, hope I shall not do so again." Numerous other entries also show that he fell short of his own expectations - "got very tipsy", "got almost fresh", "I was quite fresh" and "spent the evening in a disorderly way at J.Spencers with Sturkey etc."

Duty went hand in hand with pleasure so a December day in 1823 was spent hunting in Welland and viewing land in Storridge:

> "A bay fox turned out at Dainmoor. a very poor run. Went with Mr.Rayer to the Halesend to see the Farm."

He was essentially quite a serious young man, already showing the critical faculties that were to make him a prominent local figure and respected valuer of land and stock:

> "1st January 1823. Agriculture is at this time in a more depressed state if possible than at this time last year, wheat averaging this week but 4/8d per bushel."
> "15th September the Bannut Tree Farm let by auction at the Feathers to W. Smith the Gloucester carrier for £100 per year. A damned fool."

Buying and selling took up much of his time and he travelled to various market towns, which presented the usual hazards of crowded places: on 26th June "Mr. Twinberrow had his pocket picked of £14" - a very large sum - at Pershore Fair. His diary for a few days in May gives some indication of Lane's journeys and dealings:

> "12th May. Went to Ledbury Fair. Sold 3cwt of Cheese 2 meal at 50/- per cwt. Went afterwards to Swinley to rook shooting got quite fresh....
> 15th Went to Upton Market. Spent the evening at Hillend...
> 16th My birthday. Went to a sale at the Feathers of Land at Hollybed. Richard Cross very troublesome.
> 17th Went to Glocester Market. Sold Mr. Frewster of Nailsworth 40

bags of wheat at 8/- per bushel. bought a dozen of glasses 17/- and a dozen of knives and forks at 16/-. Called at Swinley."

Swinley seems to have been the home of his grandmother: frequent mention of it therefore indicates the characteristic commitment to family duties that he showed throughout his life.

There were, too, local civil and ecclesiastical duties which eventually he was to shoulder as an elected parish officer. As a young farmer he merely attended the springtime annual parish meeting in Castlemorton church to help elect the overseers and churchwardens, a task pleasantly followed by a lengthy visit to the Feathers until 3 o'clock.

The office of overseer was very important, carrying heavy responsibility. Until 1834 all poor relief was organised on a parochial level, each parish choosing two substantial property owners to serve as unpaid overseers who had to collect the poor rates from householders naturally reluctant to part with their money. Almost as difficult was the task of distributing these funds in a fair manner to the poor who sought help in an age where poverty was often perceived as a crime rather than a misfortune. Paupers seeking relief were not always given cash - some were sent off with nothing and others might be given cash or goods in kind. Coal, flour, shoes for the children, clothes to enable the family to seek work, extra food for a sick wife - all these and other grants might be made, but they *were* grants and not the rights which inhabitants of a modern welfare state now expect. "Going on the parish" was a humiliating experience for those seeking help, but at least in many a rural parish there was often genuine care and concern for neighbours, and a shrewd appraisal of what was the most appropriate form of help.

At the parish meeting two churchwardens would also be appointed, one to represent the parishioners and the other to represent the parson. Sometimes negotiation was necessary, the annual collection of tithes being a particularly fraught business. The local vicar or rector was still paid directly by his flock, who paid him a tithe or tenth of their income. This was still often paid in crops or other produce, though commutation to a cash payment was becoming a more practical method of payment, if little less acrimonious. Relationships between clergy and congregation sometimes lacked the Christian charity which might have been expected. On 7th May John Rayer Lane "went with Mr. Hill to meet Wm. Crewe at Rev. Mr. Thomas's to discontinue his curacy. Mrs. Garlic gave both a roasting." Even without any further details, it is not too imagine the scene: it was a foretaste of the long and bitter disagreement with the Castlemorton clergy which coloured the closing years of Lane's life.

Although John Rayer Lane was already playing his part as a pillar of the establishment, sometimes his youth got the better of him. On 25th April he "went to Mr. Cross's to collect taxes with John Rayer. We drank 9 quarts of cyder. J. Rayer quite fresh." Things seemed better organised on 28th: "Went to 45 houses to gather taxes. Drank one pint of ale and received 48/- - good afternoon's work."

Among the special occasions were the singing feast at Little Welland - "stay'd till daylight" - and, even more exciting, "Madame Tussaud's collection of wax work figures - very fine sight" seen on a visit to Worcester in June 1823. Welland Wake and races on the course near Danemoor Cross attracted an "uncommon large company" at the end of July and a new grandstand was opened in August at Worcester racecourse where there was the "largest company I ever saw." Presumably for this occasion he wore his "new bottle green coat, drab waistcoat and new hatt galon" which had cost him 30 shillings. A few days later there were races at Newent, "the first time I ever was at Newent." Ledbury races were "capital fun" in September.

He also saw plays in Worcester and Tewkesbury, breaking up the tedium of a long haymaking season. On 14th September he was at Eldersfield Church for a charity sermon; there was some good singing, though it clearly needed stamina - "one anthem lasted an hour". He then spent the evening at Moor Court in the company of Elizabeth Clarke. A few days later he went with his usual band of young friends to Worcester Fair, where they stayed late and drank. Unfortunately, on the way home, "W. Davis fell off his horse at Powick, carried him to the blacksmiths at Stanbrook and put him to bed. I was quite fresh." Next week at Upton Fair he "got quite moozy" at the Lion.

Upton Mop again took place in October 1823 and he hired a carter, George Ganderton, for £3. 10. 0 a year. Before doing so he was able to organise some entertainment, though felt cheated by the time the event was over:

> "6th October Agreed with Johnson the pugilist to let Jordan and Wheeler fight in the Hill at Malvern.
> 7th Oct. Johnson came and we staked out the ground. I went to Upton and agreed to take £4 for the use of the ground. Mr. Harris collected £7.6s at Creeses Gate. Upwards of 3000 people there before 3 o'clock

*from Worcester, Gloster, Tewksbury, Ledbury, Cheltenham.
At 4 o'clock the Fight between Jordan the Worcester man and Wheeler the Gloucester man commenced. They fought 12 rounds in 11 minutes ½ minute time for 60 guineas.
N.B. A complete Cross. Jordan the champion. Wheeler sold the battle for £50 a dead robbery.
Jack Lidiard and Barnett a Worcester youth fought a good battle.
N.B. They went to work like men.
Upon the whole very little damage done to the ground or fences."*

As a second son, he was presumably keen to find his own farm, because the Hurst was not big enough to occupy all three of the Lane sons. On 1st May 1823 he had recorded a significant event in his life:

"Mr. Watson came to put up some land marks etc. Gave me the offer of Cutlers farm, in case the present tenant left."

Cutlers was next to his home at the Hurst. On 9th December he

"went to Mr. Watson's - had the refusal of Cutlers Farm."

CUTLERS FARM CASTLEMORTON

15

On 29th December

> *"Mr. Watson and Mr. Rayer met at the Hurst. Went with me and Mr. Sturkey over Cutlers Farm, returned to the Hurst when I in conjunction with Mr Rayer took the above Farm for 3 years commencing at Candlemas 1824. Pray God prosper it."*

The Almighty seems indeed to have done so. When Lane died in 1871 at the age of 73 he was one of the most significant parishioners in Castlemorton - and still at Cutlers after more than 47 years.

Chapter Two 1845-1848
The Respected Farmer

It is particularly sad that John Rayer Lane's diaries for the period 1824 to 1845 are missing, as there is no personal record of his marriage to Elizabeth Clarke of Moor Court, Pendock in November 1825. By nineteenth century standards, Elizabeth was quite old to be having her first child at the age of 40 but they had two sons, John and William, and a daughter, Ann. The missing diaries may have shown the 1820s as the happiest time of Lane's life but it is clear that the late 1830s could not have been: in 1837 his sister Charlotte died at the age of 36, in 1838 his youngest sister Susanna died aged only 26 and in 1839 his elder brother William died at the age of 43. To have lost 3 close relatives in three successive years must have caused him to consider his own mortality.

By 1845, when the next surviving diary commences, he was in his mid-forties and a key figure in Castlemorton and neighbouring parishes: farmer of a considerable acreage, an established judge of livestock, a respected estate valuer and an informed, if biased, observer of the political scene. 1845 saw "that mischievous body, the Anti-Corn Law League" seeking the repeal of the Corn Laws which since 1815 had protected English farmers by imposing duties on foreign corn imported into this country. The effects of these laws included keeping up the price of corn - and hence of bread - to levels which caused many people living in poverty to go hungry. But Lane was convinced that the Corn Laws should remain, writing at the end of 1845:

> *"The Farm Labourers I am happy to say were never more employed, and at good wages too, and Manufacturers of all descriptions were never in a more flourishing condition - what a pity their minds should be poisoned against their best friends the Landed interest by a set of false vagabonds may they soon open their eyes and know their real Friends."*

His rise in the social scale, the problems of the Tory government and his interest in politics are all indicated by entries in December 1845 when he entertained to lunch so important a local figure as Earl Somers of Eastnor Castle and his land steward who lived at Bronsil:

> *"13th Earl Somers and Mr Watson lunched at Cutlers. His lordship called to tell me of the resignation of ministers and of the distress of his tenant J Grove and offered me the Farm for any friend of mine."*

BRONSIL

The letting of the farm progressed the next week:

> *"22nd Went with Francis Green to Bronsil - followed Mr. Watson to the Castle - met with Earl Somers and Mr. W. who gave Mr. G the refusal of Hillend Farm, the rent £300 a year - his Lordship seems determined that Mr. Grove shall quit. Dined with Mr. John Lane etc at the Castle."*

Mr. Watson seems to have succeeded his late father as steward of the extensive Eastnor estate. A presentation was to be made in recognition of the father's long service. John Rayer Lane had to help with this, recording the details at the same time as the national news:

> *"23rd Went to Ledbury on Mrs. Watson's Plate business - arranged for Mr. Wood to present it - I having declined that hon. office. Saw Earl*

> *Somers who told me Sir Robert Peel had again accepted Office."*

In February 1846 the unhappy widow was presented

> *"with a Tea Service of Silver plate value about 80£ subscribed for by the tenantry (of Earl Somers) and friends of the late George Watson Esq. Mrs. Watson in a very low and nervous way."*

At this period in the mid-19th century the development of a railway network was even more controversial than motorways are today. The nation's social and commercial life was to be transformed by it but the lines cut across farmland while the rough and ready navigators who built them were regarded with deep suspicion. The noise of the trains was believed to be acutely distressing to livestock and some people even argued that the human frame would not be able to withstand travelling at a speed of over 30 miles an hour. In October 1845 Lane's grumble was more prosaic:

> *"For the last three weeks have been continually annoyed by Persons measuring and levelling across my grounds for a line of railroad from Worcester to Gloster. 4 lines proposed."*

At the end of 1845, as railways began to criss-cross the countryside, he was convinced that

> *"This year will be noted in history for one thing, 'the Railway Mania' which has raged to an extent never before known, the Deposits of Plans the 30th November last contained speculations in these projects to the Amount of seven hundred millions!!! several lines have been projected which come through Castlemorton and one, the W.H.R & G, will be presented to Parliament."*

Like most who started by complaining about the railways, he and his family later became regular users of them as they "trained" from Malvern Wells or Upton.

His elder son, John, went off for eight days in October 1845 to serve in the cavalry - a duty which, like many young men of his class, he did most years. The younger son, William, was still attending Colwall school as a boarder in the 1840s but came home from time to time. With other members of the family William went to see the military reviews at Kempsey and Malvern. The troops in their colourful uniforms maintained the still popular image of soldiering as a romantic occupation. The British under their new young queen, Victoria, were taking care that no more Napoleons would dare to challenge this island's power. Professional soldiers went abroad to ensure that generations of schoolchildren would see a world map dominated by the pink which indicated British control and white supremacy: the British Empire was being formed.

Although John Rayer Lane was interested in national affairs his real passion was for his own district and farming activities naturally occupied much of his time: he needed no detail or explanation when he jotted brief diary entries which served simply to remind him when a job was done. Today, when most of the population live in towns, some explanation may be necessary, though we may still draw the wrong conclusions. For example, "John and I cut the lambs, 53", may mean that their tails were docked, but may well be a euphemism for castrating them. "Alfred brought the Bull to Cutlers" to perform its natural and very important duty of mating with the cows - no artificial insemination in those days. Wise farmers and their labourers have always treated animals with respect - or at least caution: in June 1847, "My wild cow tossed Rd. Price and his boy taking her to Ledbury and hurt them both."

Calves had to be earmarked for identification - especially if they strayed. Even so, the Lanes lost one of their steers at Tewkesbury in October 1845 and were unable to find it. It became the practice to "nerve" calves against murrain, a doom-laden word used to describe a number of symptoms found in unspecified diseases; although the process of nerving is not clear, any serious disease in his stock could obviously ruin a farmer, so it was well worth trying any new idea which might work, and Lane was always alive to new thinking. In November 1845 he notes his first use of a seven furrow drill at Cutlers - presumably a saving of time and labour.

Sheep had to be dipped, sheared and generally supervised, especially at lambing time. Their wool was sold to local dealers who travelled round the farms; "Martin Ganderton called and bought mine and mother's wool at 13d a lb." Lane regularly visited his mother, who continued to live nearby at the Hurst until her death in 1863 when her farm was taken over by Alfred Lane, John Rayer Lane's brother.

Post and rail fencing was not the norm, so livestock farming created a need for stock-proof hedges: an important part of the winter's work was laying hedges to regenerate them by partially cutting and pegging the branches in a nearly horizontal position - sadly a skill rarely practised today. Another uncomfortable labour was the digging out by hand of ditches to ensure proper drainage.

Lane's farming activities were very mixed, including arable as well as livestock. Ploughing, sowing and reaping each had their season but, since the weather dictated the conditions, it was never possible to predict exactly when they would take place. The most important crops for Lane were beans, barley and wheat which in the winter months, when poor weather might make it impractical to work on the land, would be threshed and winnowed indoors to separate the grain from the chaff. Lane did not mention the use of steam power for such tedious tasks until the 1850s. As the new inventions appeared, farmers tended to try them out by borrowing them from richer farmers who were prepared to experiment. Only when convinced of their worth would they risk their own money.

Much of Lane's produce was sold in the local markets but he does not seem to have sold his clover and hay, presumably needing it all for his own animals. Rick building and thatching - in those days before polythene sheets and old tyres - were skills vital to the protection of winter supplies when livestock had to be brought indoors if the weather was very cold. Even if kept outside, animals would need to eat much more than the sparse amounts of winter grass to be found growing in the fields.

Shooting provided sport and sometimes it supplemented the diet. Occasional gifts of game were received from Earl Somers or Earl Beauchamp, who enjoyed country pursuits in Castlemorton. There is quite frequent mention of pheasant, partridge and rabbits being shot. But the regular rook-shooting was simply to get rid of pests.

In August 1846 bees were causing a nuisance in the chimney at Cutlers. Today we might call in the council pest control officers. John Rayer Lane called in "Tainton and Jeynes" who "took one and a half hundredweight of honey from behind our kitchen chimney, the bees having been there for many years."

In April 1847, with his son John and 5 of the labourers, he worked at cleaning out the mud from Keyses Pool, making no mention of a phenomenon which accompanied this task many years later, when half a hundredweight of eels were removed along with the mud.

21

Opportunities for jollification were eagerly sought so, for example, regular peafeasts took place, like the one (which Lane found dull) at Hanley Quay in July 1846, a time when there was a thriving river trade: Hanley Castle's Quay Lane carried traffic to and from the quay, and the pub at the bottom of the lane did a good trade. There were annual races at Welland and Upton as well as the bigger race meetings at nearby towns like Worcester. In December 1846 he

> *"went to see Hughes Mammoth Establishment at Upton, the grandest procession I ever see, the Dragon chariot drawn by 3 camels and the Rath by 2 elephants. Dined at Mr. D. Davis's and saw the circus twice, the performance very fair."*

Today this would be regarded as politically incorrect, like "Saw a Fat Girl at a Show" in October 1846 or hearing the "Ethiopian melodists, 5 funny niggers or darkies being Englishmen" at Upton Fair the following March. Likewise, a day at Ledbury Fair combining work and play, made fun of someone's weight:

> *"Ledbury Fair. Sold 8 fresh steers at £15.5. each, brought a lame one back. Dined at the Feathers and lost a bottle on Mr. J. Brown's weight. John behaved badly in getting intoxicated."*

Young John Lane seems to have been his father's son!

BOTTOM OF HANLEY QUAY LANE

Mrs. Lane seems rarely to have accompanied her husband on these occasions, though she sometimes walked with him to the outlying farms when he went to supervise the work. One of his rare references to her was in March 1847 when "A flash woman called and obtained a quantity of bed feathers off Mrs. L. in exchange for new dresses - a dead take in." Poor Mrs. L seems to have led a dull life.

But her husband's was full of interest. A week after the "flash woman" episode he was invited to breakfast at Chambers Court by E.G. Stone, Esq., the High Sheriff.

> "About 120 horsemen and upwards of 50 carriages there - the most splendid set out I ever did see - accompanied him as High Sheriff of the county in procession reaching nearly a mile. Left them at Stoke and John joined them. Dined and drank wine at Thos. Farrs.....Spent a miserable night with Mrs. L. in consequence of John not coming home till 5 o'clock next morning."

Soon after this he took delivery of a new gig, of which he was obviously extremely proud, frequently mentioning its use for his numerous journeys.

Farmers were expected to give their labourers treats on special occasions, such as the harvest home supper in thanks for the hard work of getting in the crops without which the farm would collapse. On Christmas Day, too, the men were always given a good meal with tobacco and drink - wives and families seem not to have been included, unless his annual entry of "dined my men" followed the early principle of census-taking which in 1676 recorded that Welland's population was "72 men besides women and children."

Lane's keen mind meant that he was quick to seize any opportunity to find out what was going on around him. He therefore provides us with local evidence of a part of our national history - a vital role for local chroniclers. He knew about the attempts of the Chartists to improve the lot of working men: their six-point Charter demanded radical electoral reform to enable even poor men to vote and to sit in the House of Commons. The Chartist Land Company had also built houses on smallholdings allocated to a few lucky working men, and Lane was fascinated when he accepted the opportunity to inspect their estate at nearby Lowbands. Many of those houses, much modernised, may still be seen today. He met the leader of the movement, Feargus O'Connor, and was favourably impressed by the "visionary project." He thoroughly approved of the 44 "very neat cottages and a very handsome school building" and of "22 of the best horses I ever saw on one farm." In August 1847 the Chartists staged a demonstration at Redmarley. "About 5 or 6000 there. Nearly 200 carriages

23

came through Castlemorton. Very wet day - poor devils!" But, steeped in the traditional beliefs of the middle class landowner, he was not so much a radical as an interested observer of a new phenomenon: actually to give the vote to working men, as the Chartists demanded, was unlikely to be a scheme of which he would have approved.

In November 1846 he paid one of his frequent visits to the Pheasant and met "an excavator...who showed me some curious Roman coins." This was a few months before the discovery of a hoard of coins close to the main road in Little Malvern. In the casual attitude to archaeology which then prevailed, these found their way all over the country by means of the new postal system - the penny post system was introduced in 1840 - and thus destroyed what today would be recognised as an important never-to-be fragmented collection.

Another difference from today was in medical care. Doctors, who were much respected, actually knew very little. Their standard remedies for almost all ills were purging and bleeding, both of which often made the patient even weaker. In December 1846 Lane went to see elderly Mr. Rayer at Hillworth House and was shocked to find that he had just had

> "a most dreadful fall on the ice. Knocked out 2 of his teeth and bruised the back of his head. He was scarcely conscious for 3 hours. Sent for Mr. Braddon who bled him and put him to bed."

Despite the bleeding, Rayer obviously recovered enough to show Lane "Mr. Wedgwood's letter appointing me receiver of his Rent Charges in this parish." This was time-consuming, but was the sort of work Lane loved: the rents were collected regularly in local hostelries, where he could keep abreast of all the latest gossip. It also gave him stature among his neighbours, at a time when more and more parish responsibilities were falling on him.

In February 1846 the vicar had left the parish, his departure curtly noted:

> "I hope our exchange is for the better
> ...Paris served 6 years and left little regretted."

Although Lane liked the new vicar, the Rev. Richard Holmes, and made him very welcome at Cutlers, Holmes' plan to remove the pulpit never found favour with him. Lane seems to have been at his most dominant at a meeting concerned with this subject in November 1847 when he was the only one who argued against the plan and yet

> *"prevailed upon Mr. Holmes not to enter this meeting in the parish book as he was well beaten and I did not like to expose him....this matter I now hope is set at rest for some time to come."*

Lane was clearly a man to have on your side rather than ranged against you! Nevertheless, when a village school was planned for Castlemorton in 1847, his caustic prediction that it looked like costing three times more than necessary seems to have been ignored.

Feb: 1. 1848 Mr. Holmes called and drank Tea & Gin & water till 9

2 Have been 98 times to Netherton since this day last year

3 Went to Upton Market Dined with a Party of 16 at Gurney's the Cross Keys Inn viz Messrs B Kent Goodman T Walker &c &c Spent Evening & 10/ there

4 My Nephews & Nieces viz 6 Clarkes from Whitefields & 2 from Holdfast and 6 Hawkins's Jn. Smith Alfred & Ann Lane spent the Night at Cutters Dancing & Card playing

5 John Lane Junr. attains his Majority this day all the young Clarkes, Alfred & Ann Lane Dined and spent the Evening drank 4 Bottles Sherine

6 (Sunday) The Revd: Rd Holmes made a Birthday present to John Lane of "Clarendon's History of the Rebellion" in two very handsome Volumes — Spent the evening at the Hurst my Mothers 54th Anniversary there

7 Went in Gig to Ledbury Fair paid Hartland, Jones, Gibbs, &c asked Mr. Masefield to write to John Allen to pay me 2 yrs Tithes for late Prices Dined & drank Wine at the Feathers with Fretwell, Hickman &c

Chapter Three 1850 - 1852
A Man of the World

In 1850 Lane's life became even fuller. In August of that year he was invited to go to see Lord Somers at Eastnor Castle and

> *"received a most gratifying compliment of being recommended...as a competent person to assist Mr. William Conolly Watson during his illness as Land Steward."*

In September Watson resigned due to ill health and, in December,

> *"My very much esteemed friend Mr. William Conolly Watson after 2 years illness departed this life aged 28 universally regretted."*

As the new assistant steward, Lane was to be paid pro rata quite a high salary of £200 a year, but the real significance of his appointment was to give him the sort of opportunity he loved - to get a foot into the higher echelons of society and find out how they did things.

He had not long to wait, for on 2nd October Lord Somers' son was married. His homecoming with his bride was the local social event of the decade, and Lane was now in a position to invite various people "to meet Lord and Lady Eastnor at the Castle when they arrive home." Perhaps this was why he invested in a new pair of "button shoes...and could hardly get them off." "Great preparations...4 triumphal arches" were made for the occasion and he recorded the excitement in October 1850 as follows:

> *"19. Went this morning at 11 o'clock to Eastnor Farm. Met the Leigh and Stoulton tenantry there - above 30. Took them up to the Castle and shewed them the principal rooms - staircase - the keep - terrace - grounds - reservoir - gardens etc. till near 2 o'clock. Rode to the Hollybush turnpike with near 150 horsemen. About 3 o'clock Lord and Lady Eastnor arrived, when I shortly address'd them. Rode helter*

skelter in very quick time to the Lodge when falling in twos, rode in good order into the Castle yard. Gave 3 times 3 good cheers and was thanked by Earl Somers.

Assembled in half an hour in the Grand Drawing Room - Saloon and Library and at the sound of the Gong entered the baronial hall at 4 o'clock, where was a splendid luncheon laid, consisting of roast and boiled beef, lamb, pheasants etc. But before Grace was said Earl Somers led his beautiful daughter-in-law down the Hall followed by Lord Eastnor and Lady C. Courtenay - Rev. Courtenay and Lady Emily Cocks etc.

As Chairman of the company I proposed the following toasts with a brief preface to each - the Queen - Prince Albert etc - Earl Somers - Lord and Lady Eastnor - Countess Somers - Ladies Courtenay Prosser and E Cocks. Lord Somers in flattering language proposed my health - after which was given better health to Mr. Watson - the Leigh tenantry - the Stoulton tenantry - the Eastnor tenantry - the Town and trade of Ledbury etc. Several good songs were given and at half past 8 the meeting broke up very well pleased with the days proceedings as everything passed off pleasantly and I have no doubt will be long remembered - J. Clarke smoked a pipe with me afterwards at Cutlers.."

Two days later he was back:

"At Eastnor Castle with Lord Somers who was well pleased with the proceedings on the 19th. Lady Eastnor's picture arrived etc. Met Mr. Meates and Wm. Tempest there and agreed to let Mr. Tempest the Whitehouse Farm conditionally if his father approves of it. Dined with them at the Castle. John Lane and I had selzer water and brandy."

This will have pleased him greatly. He later went to help John Lane, the castle butler, to bottle a pipe of port in April 1851. There were "56 dozens" - a significant amount of one of his favourite drinks!

Dining at the Castle, meeting Lord Somers and being at the hub of the workings of this large estate clearly exhilarated Lane, but it took up a good deal of his time. At first he did not take kindly to the new steward, John Oakley, who came from Kent on 31st October and "appears to me to think he is the *Wise* man of Kent come down to instruct the *silly fools* of Herefordshire...I hope he will improve on a further acquaintance."

He did. He was very soon recognised as "a very quick accountant" and seems to have been shrewd enough to listen carefully and avoid confrontation. "He gave me a carte blanche to fall all the trees on Cutlers." Within a week, "I like him better." By the time of his first audit on 20th November "he seems a *jolly fellow*" though, by his own admission, Lane "drank a deal of punch" on this occasion, which may have coloured his view. In early December Oakley invited Lane to spend a week in the south-east, exploring farms in Kent and visiting London. The friendship was sealed.

The trip was minutely recorded by Lane, starting with his departure by train from Gloucester. Perhaps he even began to understand why Oakley had been rather superior in attitude, for in Kent he saw "the best hop and nut plantations I have ever seen and I think the best parish of land." Maidstone College hop garden was "the best in England." He saw a 40 foot high hawthorn hedge, beautiful hop, nut and cherry gardens and was royally entertained by Oakley's friends and relations. In London for two days, he went to the Baker Street cattle show, proudly pronouncing the Herefords to be the best cattle in the largest and best show ever held there. The two days were crammed with sights and experiences including Tussaud's waxworks, theatres, clubs, St. Paul's, the Guildhall, the Tower of London, Horseguards, the House of Commons, Westminster Abbey, Trafalgar Square with the fountains and Nelson's Column and much more: all phlegmatically summed up as "altogether a very pleasant excursion for the time of year."

The next year he went up to London again for the Great Exhibition, making the most of "the last shilling day" on 9th October and going again the next day for half a crown. The total cost of the three day visit, which included a river trip and theatre outings, was £4.6.0 but "I never did nor never shall see such an Exibition (sic) again."

The Great Exhibition, held in the "Palace of Glass" which in itself was a marvel of the age, was the brainchild of Prince Albert who was less popular than Queen Victoria would have wished for the husband she adored. It was intended to show the world the prosperity, skills and inventiveness of Britain and her growing empire. Although it turned out to be a roaring success, it was viewed with alarm and scepticism by many, who feared that it would attract crowds of undesirable characters with criminal intent. Lane himself had been rather lukewarm about it in his end-of-the-year diary entry for 1850. This is a good point at which to reproduce in its entirety one of these special entries, which always followed the same pattern of comment on life, agricultural fortunes and the political scene:

> "And thus farewell to the old Eighteen Fifty.
> May Fifty One in all things be more thrifty.

And so expires the first half of the 19th century. The last spring was cold and backward but after the middle of May vegetation made very rapid progress till the latter part of June when a frost or blight set in for a night or two and caused the whole of the grain crops to be very deficient - the wheat all over England was very much mildewed - and that with a low price is ruinous. The present price wheat 4/8 to 4/10 Barley 2/2 to 2/10 Beans and pease 3/- to 3/4. Beef and Mutton 4 to 5d per lb. These prices would not remunerate the farmer if there was no rent to be paid, how then can it be possible for the land of this country to remain in cultivation for any length of time! echo answers how?

It is an astonishing fact that the energies of the British Farmer were never more applied than at the present time altho the price of produce is so ruinously low. There is generally more money expended on the land in draining grubbing trees stocking fences etc in every direction than I ever remember before. May a time of remuneration be speedily at hand - Sir Robert Peel is no more therefore is not a subject for further abuse. Lord John Russell is still a kind of Prime Minister blown about like a feather by different contending parties, and the Parliament meets the 4th Feb.
The most prominent political event of the year has been The Pope's Bull electing Cardinal Wiseman 'Archbishop of Westminster' and a Lot of other bishops for the Romish Church. The question was simultaneously taken up and every City, Town, Village and almost every parish in England Burnt the Pope in effigy and presented addresses to the Queen on the subject. County meetings have also been held on the subject all over England, and several riots have also emanated from the same source - which prevails most Religion or Superstition in these very enlightened times?

The manufacturers have generally been prosperous through the year. but a time I fear will come when they will find to their sorrow that the Home customer is the largest and the best.

John Bull who is fond of seeing sights is to be treated in 1851 with a raree show to be held in London to be called 'The Grand Exibition' or 'the World's Fair'. What effect this will have on his *nerves I cannot tell, but however we must stuff our pockets with tin go up by cheap train rub the cobwebs out of our eyes and stare away at the grand exibition and forget the effects of Free Trade the whilst we are most enjoying it."*

These annual surveys always started with comment on the seasons and prices which obviously affected Lane's life and work. Then political comment followed, touching on a wide range of topics, which in the middle of the century included anxiety about the growing influence of Roman Catholicism, whose adherents had been granted in 1829 the civil liberties of which they had been deprived for two centuries. In this area the Hornyold family - rich landowners based in Hanley Castle - were particularly influential and, with Catholic Emancipation, they openly poured money into what they had for generations privately encouraged. New Catholic churches were built in Hanley Swan, Upton and Malvern: although Lane respected the Hornyolds as landowners, he had no love of their religion and was pleased to note in November 1850 that "Mr. Holmes gave us a sermon against Popery and meetings are being held all over England on the same subject."

In the spring of 1851 Holmes left the parish to take up the living of Eldersfield, though he and his wife maintained social contact with the Lanes. Lane himself collected Holmes' tithe rents for him at the Dragon Inn, observing that the locals were "a queer set of fellows." The Rev. John Hill came to serve Castlemorton in Holmes' place at a time when Lane was concerned about the finances:

> *"Expenses near £70 with a large sum hanging over till next year - I begin to think that a reformed management is necessary."*

He probably voiced his concern - in April 1852 he was elected churchwarden. He held the position until he died, vigilant to the last against "Romish" practices, as his later diaries show. In November 1851 he made a quaint entry, which possibly indicates local adherence to the age-old custom of taunting a bridegroom:

> *"Rev. Mr. Hill gave a Lecture before the sermon (rather unusual) about some vagabonds Tanging Jerry Taylor who was married on the 4th."*

Less than a week after being made churchwarden Lane took on another solemn duty, becoming one of the Guardians who met fortnightly to oversee instruct the *Silly Fools* of Herefordshire — time will tell I hope he will improve on a further acquaintance Dined &c with him Theatre & Tempest there

Nov. 1. 1850 went in Gig to Eastnor took Mr. Oakley to Ledbury introduced him to the Banker, Auctioneer &c Attended the Coppice Sale which sold very well Mr Oakley a very quick accountant at Ledbury till past 10 Brandy at Eastnor Farm Home by 12 —

4. Met Mr. Oakley at the Gullet took him to Mr. Wm Smiths — Mr Greenway's Chd. Beaman — Mrs Eh and & Cutters he gave me a Carte blance to fall all the trees on Cutters — went with him to Ockeridge & Netherton &c — I like him better called at the Feathers —
The 2 Misses Jew came to Cutters

5. At the Feathers this evening altow by 9. 4 Clarkes of Whitefields & Miss Ireland Mr A Clarke, 2 Jews & Alfred Sam at Cutters till 1 Oclock — 6th the same and Bess Clarke & Martha Baylis at Cutters

Nov 6 Met Mr Oakley at Netherton he goes to London tonight — B Re

9 Went to Worcester Market very flat Wheat at 15/ a Bag Rec'd 13£ off Sally King

8 Smoked a Pipe with Mr John Player B Re

10 Edw'd Knight's Ricks burnt down

11 at the Feathers this evening

13 Went to Tewkesbury Market Mutton sold George Ireland 5. 2yr old Steers at 8£ each — Paid Mr Wedgwood 265£ to Kemmersley & Co — Paid Simson for Seed Wheat — Mr Player paid for my Wine — called at the Moor Court & Supped — Ann & Miss Jews there &c —

15 Went to Eastnor Farm this Morning and commenced an Inventory and Valuation of all the Farming Stock with Mr E Baylis worked hard till night Dined & then at home by 10

16 Called at Brousil to enquire how Mr Watson is — no better — finished my Valuation at Eastnor Farm called at Netherton the Feathers &c

17 Wm Lane's 20th Birthday Mr Holmes gave us a Sermon against Popery and Meetings are being held all over England on the same subject & landwife at the House

the administration of the workhouse built in Upton in 1836 to serve the town and 22 surrounding parishes.

The Poor Law Amendment Act passed by the Whig government in 1834 had changed the system of poor relief which had operated for more than two hundred years. Although parishes were still responsible for the poor within their boundaries, the law now insisted that wherever possible they should be placed in workhouses and not given relief in their own homes. The poor found the workhouses degrading - as the government intended, in a drive to reduce the numbers seeking help. It was a long time before enlightened reformers convinced the more affluent classes that most of the poor could not help themselves and that society was failing to find them work. Meanwhile, parishes continued to elect overseers of the poor to collect the poor rates, though clearly strange appointments were occasionally made. In March 1851, for example, Lane had noted that Charles Beaman and John Bullock were appointed overseers at the annual parish meeting, "very improperly, as neither can read or write."

Despite owning a gig, he walked a great deal to his various farms and to Upton, where he would sort out a wide range of business matters after attending the guardians' meetings. He served as a guardian for 14 years, until April 1866. After the Second world war the old workhouse building became a home for the elderly and was, rather precipitately, demolished by Malvern Hills District Council in 1980, to the fury of Uptonians who had other plans for this superb example of Victorian institutional architecture.

Lane's business activities included a good deal of valuation work, sometimes as far away as the other side of Hereford, where he helped value the large estate at Arkstone Court. Closer to hand was the brickworks at Interfield, Leigh Sinton, where in January 1851 a Mr. Chamberlain said the land was "utterly unfit to make tiles." Several meetings were necessary, ending with a 6 hour marathon examining a large number of what Lane sarcastically called "gentlemen." His final biting observation was,

> "If the value of the premises is estimated according to the respectability of the witnesses the price will be very low indeed."

A much more pleasant task was looking over 40 cottage gardens in Welland to award the prize given by General Lygon. It went to Jos. Jones whose home and carefully tended garden were on the Marl Bank.

Although Lane was vividly articulate he clearly wrote his diary at speed, often neglecting his punctuation and giving rise to some ambiguities which it is impossible to resolve. For example, in May 1851, "Loaded my new blue waggon the first time Thomas Rodway has been 4 years building" seems to imply that the waggon took an inordinate time to complete. But it is possible that the reference is to some totally unrelated building work undertaken by Rodway. Quite clear, however, is his affection for "my old Mare Lively aged 26 years." She "died suddenly she has been to me a faithful slave for 24 years." In June, Lane "shore my sheep." One died after the shearing, out of a total of 129 ewes and 69 lambs. Sixty of the ewes were taken to his farm at Netherton. When he "got in a wheat rick" in July 1851, one wonders how he counted the 700 mice he claimed were in it.

By this time Lane's sons, too, were old enough to assume local responsibilities and were the enumerators for the census of March 1851, finding the parish to hold 449 males and 403 females. That last week of March was clearly quite an exciting one: he took his daughter Ann to Worcester market, where "she had her pocket picked of 2 sovereigns." Another crime occurred during the night of Good Friday 1851: "two bureaus broken and 6 or 7£ stolen - A Very Daring Burglary" at Hillworth, home of 81 year old Mr. Rayer.

The diaries also refer to local events such as the roadworks near Welland crossroads in June 1851: "50 men at work reducing the Garret pitch." Much more exciting was the collapse of Upton bridge in February 1852. Its repair had been a subject of controversy since the 17th century when it was damaged during the civil war: was it the responsibility of the people of Upton, of the county or of the trustees of the Edward Hall charity? As another 19th chronicler, Turberville, succinctly put it, the bridge concluded its own history by falling down in the floods which wreaked havoc in the whole area in the winter of 1852. Lane noted this, as he noted controversy about the design of its replacement - whether or not it should have an opening swivel section to let high-masted river traffic pass freely.

He appears not to have approved of Guy Fawkes celebrations, one ambiguous 5th November entry reading, "a Dangerous display of Fireworks this evening near the Mythe Bridge - the Gate lock spoilt and we came thro' Upton home." Did this mean that the fireworks had damaged the turnpike gate - or were the two statements unrelated?

Occasionally his jottings conjure up particularly vivid pictures, as in April 1852, when there were inquests at the Pheasant

> *"on W. Beachens who fell dead in the road and at the Feathers on Eliz. Turner who died of appoplexy in consequence of excitement caused by fighting with her sister-in-law."*

His end of the year thoughts in 1851 were especially wide ranging:

> *"Emigration, chiefly to America, is rapidly increasing and at present averages about 350,000 per annum. Gold from California and Australia is imported at the present time to the amount of £10,000,000 per annum.*
>
> *These two causes must materially affect the future prospects of society but whether for better or for worse is a problem not easily solved. Mankind seems all to be engaged in a race of competition and a tendency to gather together in large masses, the large towns and cities of this kingdom rapidly increasing in population and the agricultural districts in about the same ratio decreasing."*

Doubtless his interest in emigration was heightened by the impending departure of John William Rayer, probably his nephew, whose affairs were entrusted to Lane during his two year absence abroad. In March 1852 he was to sail from London, and Lane took him in his gig to Tewkesbury, lent him £20 and "gave him 5 shillings to be the first money spent by him in Australia." Four years later, it clearly pained him that, on his return from Australia, Rayer spent 9 weeks in the area before visiting him at Cutlers.

Chapter Four 1854-1856
The Prime of Life

The 1850s were probably the prime of John Rayer Lane's life. He had many professional interests and, living at Cutlers, he farmed about 500 scattered acres including nearby Pewtriss Farm, the Mill Farm on the road towards Gloucester and Netherton, a farm lying between Eastnor and the main Malvern to Ledbury road: in the 1840s he recorded an average of 90 visits a year to Netherton. He found it conveniently near to the Wellington Inn which until recently boasted a sign portraying the great duke after whom it was named. There is an oral tradition that flags were used to send signals from the farther flung farms to Cutlers, but the diaries make no mention of this. Although he purchased Pewtriss Farm in 1847 he did not own all this land: this was the period of large estates rented out to tenant farmers. In 1855 the Mill was taken over by his son William who was to marry Harriet Clarke in 1857 - "I wish them Health and Happiness." William, with an unfortunate reputation for being too fond of cider, never enjoyed the universal respect commanded by his father.

Vast amounts of cheese were sent to market - 6 hundredweight in May 1854 to Ledbury, and 16 hundredweight to Gloucester in October 1855 give some idea of the quantity. It is not clear where this prodigious output came from - presumably milk from all Lane's farms contributed to it.

In the nineteenth century farming was physically even harder than it is today. Lane employed up to 16 labourers who, like all farm workers, were expected to work long hours in all weathers, enduring both the blistering heat of haymaking or harvesting in summer and the biting cold of winter. On 9th February 1855, for example, Lane recorded 10 feet of snow in Cutlers Road and, on 20th February, six continuous weeks of frost. "The severest frost we have had for many years - not a drop of water left at Cutlers - takes the cows etc to Keyses Pool." The following December even the River Severn - still a major trade route - froze over. The hard weather also caused many more people to apply for poor relief, as he noted after a visit to Upton workhouse.

37

The board of Guardians of the Upton Poor Law Union met every fortnight. Four times a year they had to agree on contracts with local tradesmen for the supply of goods, representing a substantial amount of business for the successful supplier of bread, meat or whatever. Some meetings were quite acrimonious, such as when one of the guardians, the Rev. Richard Holmes, felt he must lay a charge against the medical officer, Dr. Sheward, who was eventually pronounced by the national Poor Law Board to be guilty of fraud and neglecting his duties at Eldersfield, the parish to which Holmes had gone upon leaving Castlemorton. Some guardians, however, continued to support Sheward so the atmosphere may well be imagined. In November 1855 Lane and another guardian brought a charge against Rhodes, the governor of the workhouse, for "putting a boy with the Itch in the Men's Ward." Probably Rhodes robustly defended himself by pointing out deficiencies in accommodation that forced him to do this because, two weeks later, Lane "went over the house with Drs. West, Goodman and Marsh and agreed to alter several rooms." In January 1856 Dr. Marsh was also censured for "reducing a dislocated *Elbow* instead of a *shoulder* of a woman, Page". Board meetings were at times lively affairs: that of 29th May 1856 was described by Lane himself as "very discordant." Sometimes they were followed by dinner, as on 13th July 1854: "Was chairman at dinner at Gurneys. 14 dined. Lovesey of Worcester a capital speaker there." These dinners were not necessarily for the guardians only, and the one on 30 October 1856 seems to have been a very special affair: 32 men - respectable pillars of Upton, Tewkesbury and Worcester society - drank "about 42 bottles of wine."

Interest in education was mounting at this time and two religious societies, the National Society for the Education of the Poor in the Principles of the Established Church and the non-conformist British and Foreign Society, each set up schools for working-class children in many parts of the country, hoping thereby to win converts for their respective brands of Christianity. Upton had a National School in Upton for the children of local labourers, and the Upton Union workhouse board considered the expediency of sending the workhouse children there, instead of educating them in the workhouse itself. Such a plan was more likely to please the inmates of the workhouse than respectable and socially conscious parents outside it: they would be reluctant to see their offspring rubbing shoulders with the less fortunate inhabitants of an institution which they dreaded might become their own ultimate destination. Snobbery has never been confined only to the middle and upper classes.

Middle class families like the Lanes felt confident and secure in their station in life. Family solidarity was reinforced at great gatherings like those which took place at New Year and Whitsun. Mrs. Lane's family home at Moor Court was the venue: 30 or 40 would meet there, sometimes staying overnight or sometimes driving home late, as Lane did on 1st January 1856 and "lost part of my gig lamp" - the 19th century equivalent of losing a hubcap today, but with more inconvenient consequences.

Travelling was naturally much less convenient before the invention of the motor-car, and was also more hazardous than we might suppose. In January 1855, after a "jovial evening" at Gurneys, where he was chairman of a party of 18, Lane "got home safe" even though it was a very foggy night and "my horse got off the road in Hook Common." The next night, which was especially dark, he called at the Feathers and got lost as he came along the common which he had known all his life. Journeys at night in such conditions may well have reminded him of the unfortunate Rev. Henry Fothergill, to whom a memorial was erected in Castlemorton church - he drowned one foggy winter night in 1827 when his horse stumbled in a deep water-filled pit on the road to Upton. Lane often walked, sometimes alone. In January 1856 he walked home with his son John after staying until 11 o'clock with Colwall farmers at the Jockey. Like all countrymen, he was observant of the scene around him, day or night, and in August 1856 noted "a beautiful lunar rainbow."

Social convention was a strict dictator and rarely more so than in matters concerning death. In July 1854 Lane's relative, John Rayer, was married and made his first public appearance with his bride on the anniversary of his grandfather's death. This first public appearance of newly-weds always attracted attention to them and although the Rayers' appearance was in church - what could be more respectable? - for it to occur on that anniversary was considered by Lane to be in poor taste.

"My old and much esteemed friend, John Clarke Esq. Solicitor, of Upton aged 75" who died in May 1854 may well have been the brother of Lane's wife. Whether or not this was the case, his tribute was unequivocal:

> *"his unobtrusive manners and kind disposition made him a favourite with all, as was this day evinced by the closing of every shop window in town. The pallbearers were myself and G.L.Piercy, Mr. Thomas Walker and Thomas Bird and the Revs. Grice and Philpotts."*

Mr. Walker, one of these pallbearers, was himself deeply respected by Uptonians. A young solicitor in Upton at the time of the 1832 cholera outbreak, he had been so caring towards victims of this dreaded disease, entering their infected homes and giving them practical help, that thirty years later, in 1864, the rector's wife, Emily Lawson, paid tribute to his courage and devotion in her fascinating history of the town.

A few days after the Clarke funeral, at the Sunday service,

> *"some extra singers at our church sung Funeral pieces supposed to be for the late Mrs. Hill (late of Hillend, a kindhearted woman) but their family was not there - I had a black scarf and hatband on and that was enough."*

Clearly, social obligations were a minefield - if the family *had* been there, perhaps it would have been an *appearance* in poor taste!

In the summer of 1854 Lane helped two women to draw up their wills, further evidence of the wide range of work he was called upon to undertake. The first was Ann Hart, "my steady housekeeper at the Mill...a very honest woman" who died in the September. The other was Mrs. Homan, who seems to have been a woman who died in March 1855 and about whom Lane wrote the following interesting comment:

> *"Attended the Funeral of the Late Mrs. Sarah Homan aged 86 to Welland Church on Horsback as Pallbearer with Mr. W Davis F Ward and G Jones. Thos. Holland Solr and Dr. Goodman etc.During the life of her first husband Rich. Harris she was pretty well respected but for the last 26 years since his death she has acted in a very extraordinary way tyrannical, litigious, vindictive and mean to a degree, supposed to be worth some 15 or 16,000£ some few years ago; I now doubt whether her Estate will pay 20/- in the £ all spent in Litigation."*

Lane enjoyed the occasional lecture such as that in May 1856 when, in Upton Town Hall, the lecturer on mesmerism had "complete and unreserved power over" 5 people, the effect being "most ludicrously astonishing." During the 19th century several new clubs and institutions appeared but most of their lectures and activities were more staid than this. A Mechanics Institute was founded in Upton for working men, and in April 1855 Lane *"attended a concert at the Town Hall for the benefit of the Mechanics Institute. Eleven performers from Worcester, very well performed. Mr. Symonds made an excellent address - the room very much crowded."*

The Rev. W. S. Symonds was rector of Pendock for 42 years and a versatile character. A keen local historian and naturalist, he wrote the historical novels, *Malvern Chase* and *Hanley Castle* as well as material on geology and natural history. When he died in 1887 aged 68 he was survived by nearly twenty years by Hyacinth, immortalised in his 1883 dedication of *Hanley Castle* as "for more than forty years my good wife and true". In 1855 he was in his mid-thirties and frequently met Lane at family parties and other social occasions.

There was robust entertainment for men, while women tended to less strenuous activities, confined by social convention as much as their clothing. Lane's daughter Ann went to the occasional ball and also to a bazaar in Ledbury to raise money for the restoration of the ancient chapel dedicated to St. Katherine. In August 1854, with her aunt (presumably as chaperone) and two female friends she "went by Railway from Tewkesbury to Teignmouth for a week's sea-bathing" but actually stayed for three weeks - one of her rare holidays, and probably remembered for the rest of her rather uneventful life.

Her father "saw a fellow walk 7 miles in 57 minutes" at Upton and a little later "attended the Eastnor Coursing Meeting. 33 courses, 14 hares - plenty of dogs - very wet." Afterwards 52 dined at the Somers Arms in Eastnor, a "very jolly evening" which lasted until 2 o'clock. The Somers Arms was also the venue for the rent audit, when

SOMERS ARMS HOTEL. EASTNOR

> *"Mr. Thorold made a speech to give all the tenants Lord Somers permission to Gin all the hares and rabbits....John drank rather too much gin and water."*

Mr. Thorold's witty use of the ambiguous word "gin" - meaning both a trap and alcohol - was "received with much applause." In March 1855 Lane went to Pull Court, home of the Dowdeswells, for a public breakfast at 8 o'clock. There were 500 people who then escorted

> *"Mr. William Dowdeswell, High Sheriff, to Worcester to meet the judges at half past 12 but they did not arrive till past 6 o'clock."*

The breakfast must have seemed a long time ago!

Much of Lane's social life centred on the village inns, such as the Feathers, which was run until October 1855 by Charles Beaman and his wife. When Thomas Taylor took over, Lane wrote that he doubted that the Beamans "will not find retirement so pleasant as dropping coppers into the till - time will tell." Notwithstanding this caustic comment, he felt enough regard for them to take them a goose when they had been in their new home a few days. In February 1856 M. Gregorie, a French strong man, attracted 100 people to the Pheasant, breaking stone and iron with his fist.

Upton and Ledbury offered a greater choice of food, and when Lane went to see Masefield, the Ledbury solicitor, or did business at Ledbury market he normally ate well: "Turbutt and haunch venison" were a cut above the local offerings.

In June 1855 Lane attended a meeting of the Malvern, Woolhope and Cotswold Field Clubs at Great Malvern, and heard Sir Roderick Murchison's lecture on the Worcestershire Beacon.

> *"Dined at 5 at the Abbey Boarding House with more than 100 scientific philosophers...spent about three hours there very pleasantly hearing speeches etc. 2 brandy and cigars at the Belle Vue."*

The "Malvern Monster Bonfire" was lit on the Worcestershire Beacon in January 1856 and dismissed by Lane as a failure, visible at Upton but not at Worcester. Those who observed it more closely on the hill itself had to contend with wind, snow, ice and dense clouds of smoke as they bravely tried to celebrate the fact that Malvern had the most modern amenity available - a gas supply. Another new invention was photography and in June 1856 Lane "had my *Likeness* taken by the Collodion photographic process." Sadly, this picture has been lost.

The outside world made little impact on rural Worcestershire but Lane continued to be conscious of nationally significant events and was troubled by the Crimean War in 1854-6. In October 1854 he heard news that the great Russian stronghold of Sebastopol had been taken, but in fact a great deal more fighting was to occur. By December he and the Rev. John Hill were going "round the parish to collect subscriptions for the Patriotic Fund for the relief of soldiers widows and children." They collected the surprisingly large sum of £10.3.0d. The distant war had caught the imagination and sympathy of the people, encouraged by *The Times* to pin the blame where it belonged. Lane's end-of-year survey reflected widespread dissatisfaction with government conduct of a war which, most unusually, was to immortalise a woman - Florence Nightingale.

> *"To describe exactly the Political Year would be a difficult task but to state generally as before said we began in Peace and ended in War with the Emperor of Russia... our Army with that of our Allies the French landed in the Crimea in September, and since that, to the present time have suffered unknown hardships owing to the mismanagement of our Government at home in not sending supplies of food, clothing etc altho several of the bloodiest battles ever recorded have been fought viz the Alma - Inkerman - Balaclava. The Allied army are now and have been for 4 months lying before Sebastopol and hammering away at that almost impregnable Fortress. Poor fellows I wish them safe at home. The sympathy of the British public has never been so excited as it has lately been on behalf of these poor sufferers and their widows and orphans, the subscriptions are immense but at present the amount not known. Pray God send Peace. I anticipate that the year we are now entering on will be one of unparallelled interest in an historical point of view and changes take place the consequences and effect of which no mortal man can foretell."*

At the same time he expressed thanks that the latest outbreak of cholera, which had first arrived in England in 1831 and devastated Upton in 1832, seemed to be over. A cure for - and indeed, the cause of - this dreaded disease had yet to be discovered.

> "That dreadful scourge the Cholera has through the year made sad ravages through various parts of England but is now, thank God, nearly extinct."

Medical knowledge remained limited: poor Mrs. Rodway, who died in September 1855 was "Tapped 40 times." This sounds very uncomfortable and presumably means drawing fluid from some site of infection.

The Crimean war dragged on. In March 1855 there was a

> "Humiliation and Fast Day on account of the war or more truly the Mismanagement of our government."

At the end of 1855 Lane lamented that

> "many of our brave countrymen have found soldiers graves in that inhospitable land... Lord Palmerston is still at the head of affairs if any head it has, for it is generally considered that this is the weakest ministry ever known and the emergency is the greatest."

When at last peace came in 1856 a public holiday was declared and there was a "Crimean heroes banquet" at Ledbury.

> "The grandest dinner I ever attended. 6 officers treated...room beautifully decorated. About 60 ladies in the gallery - 5 singers from Worcester...not home till 4 next morning."

Where, one wonders, was the common soldier? What lessons had been learned about war? It all seems a chilling rehearsal for the even more terrible bloodbath of the First World War, when the comfortable middle-aged and middle class despatched a whole generation of young men to die in a relentless war of attrition.

The 19th century was a time of harsh punishment, even after the banning of the terrible man-traps designed to deter poachers. In July 1855 Lane's brother went to Worcester sessions "to give John Smith's character, who is to have 12 months hard labour for stealing 7 sheep off Mr. Wm. Lane of Chaceley." Alfred Lane's intervention appears to be in defence of Smith but we do not know if it affected his punishment.

By the middle of the 19th century enclosure was occurring all over the countryside, bringing into private ownership the common land which had for centuries been used by locals for grazing and other purposes. The loss of common rights hit poorer people hard for they had been used to burning windfall wood as fuel or picking fruit and nuts to eke out their monotonous and meagre diet. The greatest benefit of all was the right to graze animals which would provide milk, cheese or meat.

But enclosure appealed to the richer landowners who were eager to farm more productively, using new farming methods such as selective breeding. Such practices were impossible when animals were jumbled up together on the great tracts of common land which the rich and influential yearned to use more efficiently. It was they who secured Acts of Parliament to permit enclosure. Parishes were surveyed and the common land was allocated to local landowners in a manner proportionate to the property they owned. Ascertaining the precise rights of each local property owner provided good pickings for the lawyers while land measurement and valuation put power into the hands of the valuers. The rich, who owned a large acreage, got most. The poor, baffled by the entire process, got least and often, unable to afford the necessary hedging and fencing of their small share of land, gave up and sold it to the richer farmers who employed them as labourers.

So divisions between rich and poor were emphasised, causing enclosure to have a dramatic effect on rural society in the 19th century. In neighbouring Hanley and Welland the common land virtually disappeared: in Hanley the influence of

THE PHEASANT AT WELLAND

the Hornyold and Lechmere families was reinforced, together with that of the church; in Welland it heralded the removal of the focal point of the parish to the cross-roads by the Pheasant Inn. John Rayer Lane expressed some misgivings about the enclosure of Welland in 1847; it had less impact in his own parish of Castlemorton, where hundreds of acres under the jurisdiction of the Ecclesiastical Commissioners remained unenclosed. In the mid-20th century this land came under the control of the Malvern Hills Conservators, whose *raison d'etre* was the preservation of common land, so Castlemorton Common remains today in much the same state as it has been for centuries.

The enclosure of Ripple and Upton-on-Severn in 1863 had important consequences for their inhabitants - and a significant effect on John Rayer Lane. In May 1856 he was elected unopposed as valuer and surveyor for Upton's enclosure process. Shrewd as ever, he had few illusions:

> *"I hope and trust that at the finish of this arduous and responsible undertaking I may deserve as much popularity as I seem now to have."*

Chapter Five 1857-1859
A Pillar of the Community

During the mid 1850s John Rayer Lane was very much in demand: unpaid responsibilities as churchwarden and poor law guardian took up many hours a month on top of an increasing amount of paid work. His diary is packed with entries reflecting a richly varied range of interests and responsibilities. An important local figure who had achieved from modest beginnings an enviable reputation, he kept both mind and body very active at a stage in life when many would be seeking a reduced work-load.

His labours as surveyor and valuer for Upton and Ripple Enclosure began in the summer of 1856 and occupied much of 1857 and 1858. Meetings were held at the White Lion in Upton so that parishioners could stake their claims: 81 did so at the first meeting and 17 at the second. All these claims had to be considered, to ascertain which were valid. In May 1857 a meeting to hear 30 objections lasted for 5 hours; that of Thomas Charles Hornyold was "the only one of importance" and the meeting adjourned for a month so that it might be considered more carefully. The adjourned meeting was "a roomful from 10 till half-past one. Mr. Thomas Holland called several witnesses who *proved that he was very silly."* This is another of Lane's ambiguities - was it Hornyold or Holland who was silly? Since Hornyold was widely respected and Holland was one of Lane's least favourite lawyers, it would have pleased him greatly if Holland was made to look foolish and this is the likeliest interpretation. After this meeting Lane dined with a friend and they drank "3 bottles of good old port...and...smoked at the Crown, both my customers *slewd up."*

Although much of the lengthy task of valuing Upton and Ripple took place in crowded, stuffy rooms, it also involved tramping the fields to measure them and assess their quality. The pleasure of this outside activity was occasionally further enhanced by interesting phenomena, like the "eclipse of the sun, the *nearest to a total* I have ever seen" which took place on the day he started from Welland's old school near Welland Court on the Welland-Upton boundary to value 370 acres through the Stanks, Wheatley Lane and Lockeridge. When the

47

land was divided up into allotments for private ownership he and other officials had to pay careful attention to an important requirement of any enclosure Act - the provision of a satisfactory amount of land for public purposes. This meant not only ensuring a proper road network to give access to the newly created fields, but also taking the unprecedented - and unlikely to be repeated - opportunity of choosing the most appropriate sites for laying out amenities such as a cemetery, recreation area and allotments for the poor to grow vegetables. Such facilities might be viewed as sops to placate the poor who felt aggrieved by the loss of valuable common rights. The closure of old footpaths was another difficult problem: the respect - and the thick skin - he had developed during his years as a valuer were vital when dealing with pressure from all sides. He deposited "plans and specifications for roads, brooks etc" at the White Lion in early December. The work must have seemed endless as each stage in the enclosure process inexorably demanded attention. In September 1858 allotments were staked out to be sold in November, and by December we find references to the people who did particularly well out of the whole business: "All the lawyers very busy" wrote Lane on 28th December - and repeated it on 30th!

At the same time as the preparations for enclosure were going on, he undertook valuations connected with the building of the Worcester and Hereford Railway, the development of which necessitated proper compensation of landowners. In March 1858, for example, he went to Worcester and thence to Bransford, Powick and St. John's to survey and value tenant compensation. On this occasion he enjoyed "bread and cheese and some capital ale at the Fox and home by 6." A fortnight later he had to assess tenant compensation from the Ledbury "Tunnel to the Bush Pitch. Dined with Mr. P. Baylis who is unreasonable in his demand on the Co." It appears that the dinner did not help Baylis' case! The railway line came into use in 1861: the remarkable station - now a listed building - at Great Malvern was opened in 1862, together with the adjoining Imperial Hotel, now the main building of Malvern Girls' College.

Lane, who was an honourable man, was occasionally distressed by his work, as when he went to Birmingham in January 1858 to represent Mr Lewis T. Chambers concerning the value of land north of Birmingham. When asked to take on the case he

> *"had but little peace of mind, believing that Chambers was got into such a job as would cost him a great deal of money to get out."*

His fears were realised when he reached the land

> "*this Damd. spot 153 acres of ...the very worst ground I ever trod on - a black sterile land - we walked over it, valued stock etc for 3 hours and returned ... for dinner, wine etc. I need not record more as I shall never forget it.*"

This last sentence helps to explain why it is impossible to follow the details of the case but we know that he valued the land, generously, at £610, while the vendor's valuer put it at £2700.

> "*We had a scene. At 8 I left and went to Brookes White Hart and smoked a pleasant pipe or two. At 12 returned to the Acorn....went to bed leaving Chambers in the hands of Prideaux. No sleep, rose at 8, a cup of tea and made my escape. They had done him and got the money £300. This was the most villainous swindle I ever was concerned in.... I am truly sorry for him.*"

Chambers seems to have recovered somewhat from this blow, and three months later Lane went with him to look at Morton House Farm, Birtsmorton. He did not record the outcome.

Over the years the meetings of the board of guardians at Upton workhouse had clearly become a chore for Lane. A new workhouse governor was appointed in 1857 when Rhodes left and, after new appointments were made to the board in the spring of 1858, he made another of his withering observations, succinctly summing up the situation: "a deal of talent but little common sense in the present board." The following January there was a very long discussion about new arrangements for medical care; essentially a practical man, he dismissed it as "All theory." One suspects that by this time it was the dinner at Gurneys (e.g. "Salmon and lamb, 4/9d each") which persuaded him to continue with this otherwise tedious work.

Rent collection day was more interesting for a sociable man like Lane who was a shrewd

THE FEATHERS INN. CASTLEMORTON

49

judge of people and enjoyed being at the heart of things. It was probably the most enjoyable work he did. In January 1857, for example, he attended the Feathers to receive tithe rent charges and savour the atmosphere.

> *"A large party of the middle paymasters there. Day, Crump and Pope absent either on account of pride or poverty. A very jovial meeting, not home till past 12."*

The story continued a week later, when Crump "called and paid his tithe and smoked and told l--s." Crump came again later with more lies and by March Lane accused him of getting the parish into debt in his post as surveyor of the highways.

Reappointed Churchwarden each year, Lane repeatedly showed concern for "poor old Mr Hill", the clergyman who had "a stroke of paralysis" in February 1857. In January he "broke down" in the service and was "nearly done up" by the end of that month. When old William Clutterbuck died in 1857 and left money to buy bread for the poor at Christmas part of Lane's duties as churchwarden was to see that the terms of this and other such bequests and charities were carried out. Another duty he seemed to enjoy was the regular visitation at Worcester where churchwardens had to report to the church authorities. In May 1858 he gave Mr. Hill breakfast and took him into Worcester, where they joined representatives from other parishes. They heard the address by Archdeacon Hone, a "businesslike" man whose pronouncements always seemed to meet with Lane's approval. To this pleasure was added the satisfaction for Lane of presiding over dinner for 15 at the Bell. This, however, cost the exorbitant amount of 13/6 each, perhaps partly explained by the entry *"3 colts* (including his own son William) a bottle each."

In April 1858, aware of his heavy work-load, he recorded, "I for a wonder have been at home all this week up to the 11th." In September 1858 he declined an invitation to judge at Ledbury Fair, the sort of event in which he once would have revelled: perhaps shortage of time made him more choosy about what he took on.

At home, life seems to have changed little since his younger days: the "young ones" had their all night winter parties, as he had once done, and there were visitors from time to time, of whom he was a quick judge. Young Enoch Perrins was "a very intelligent young man", Miss Staight who drank tea in August *"has* a tongue" and he clearly had a soft spot for "little Johnny Hill", who, amongst other things, shot a brace of partridges in November 1856 and left them at Cutlers. This was the day after he recorded a great *"bustle"* at Eastnor, where Earl Somers had quarrelled with his valet - only a fortnight before they had been "amusing the neighbourhood". While affecting to consider local gossip not worth his attention, Lane delighted in knowing everything that was going on.

In October 1858 his son John and all the servants went off to Tewkesbury Fair, leaving at Cutlers only Lane himself, "Mrs. Lane, Turner and the boy." He seems to have been a fair but strict employer, many of his servants staying with him for years, though one wonders why a groom and cowman ran away in 1858. Some servants misbehaved in a manner which would not have been tolerated by any employer: in December he "turned W. Wagstaff off. He has worked for me all his life, an habitual drunkard." But, in an age where everyone knew their station in life, he faithfully fulfilled the obligations of his class to its employees, and appears not to have shortchanged them; in return he expected them to know their duties. He knew good work when he saw it and gave praise where it was due. When the pump went wrong in February 1859 the pumpmaker "put a new oak pump in and did his work well."

Without the sickly sentimentality of many Victorians, Lane had innate respect for the animals which he knew to be at the heart of any farm's success. His affection for "my old mare Flower" who got into the brook was clearly enhanced by his respect for her: "Borrowed Mr. Twinberrow's team to pull her out. She walked after to Hanley Hall."

Since the weather largely dictated the work and fortunes of the farming world, he was naturally very interested in it, recording it regularly. These comments on the weather were normally so brief and routine that they hold no particular interest for the modern reader. Nevertheless, the farmer's preoccupation with the weather needs to be recognised and, on occasion, dramatic climatic phenomena were noted by Lane. In June 1857, for example, a violent thunderstorm "struck John Gunnell's cottage, drove the window in and the dough trough *out* and broke the furniture etc." The next month, during a long hot, dry period, "several horses fell on the road loose stones poor young Castree lost his life by being thrown". A fortnight later "a beautiful 3 hours rain very beneficial."

Perhaps it was this very hot summer which led to a spectacle he witnessed the following September:

51

> *"the largest quantity of hops on waggons I ever saw in Worcester, reaching from the machine bottom of Broad Street far above the Star and Garter Foregate Street."*

He derived enormous pleasure from seeing anything unusual: another example was when his son, "fishing the Lower Pool" got "a quantity of very large eels, one weighed 3¼ lbs." He was also fascinated by a comet in 1858.

Marriage was naturally an occasion for celebration, especially if any member of a well known local family was one of the parties. A week before his son William married Harriet Clarke in November 1857 the Lanes were invited to dinner at her home, Whitefields. This appears to have been the wedding dinner, attended only by close relatives and friends: "I wish them health and happiness." After the wedding service bride and groom departed for London at 3 o'clock, and at the Mill Farm where William seems to have lived for the last couple of years, there was a "jollification" on the wedding night. The happy couple returned at 9 o'clock four days later, "the bells having been rung merrily since 4 this afternoon." Next day they made their formal appearance at church and entertained close family in the evening at the Mill Farm.

On a somewhat grander level, in October 1858 Sir E.A.H. Lechmere, leading landowner of Hanley Castle, came home after his London marriage and brief Yorkshire honeymoon.

> *"The carriage drawn by Men (quaere donkeys) from Upton Bridge to the Rhydd and Flags, Garlands, mottoes and other tomfooleries all up the road - a dinner after at Hanley Quay, tickets 4/6."*

With his dry wit Lane was quick to denounce "fooleries", even seeing them at the funeral of Thomas Charles Hornyold, the highly regarded champion of Roman Catholicism who owned Blackmore House and Park.

> *"About 200 followed and upwards of 1000 spectators. About a dozen priests and chief of the service performed by Dr. Hullathorne, Bsp. of Birmingham and all except the oration in Latin and consequently appeared to those ignorant of that Language to be a three hours of Tomfoolery."*

But he was clear-sighted enough not to confuse the outward show with inner substance so his final comment was the most telling: "I fear he will not be surpassed."

His dry, sometimes self-deprecating, humour showed again, two weeks later: "a low day for me, very wet. Gave a tramp Brown a shilling, then came Joe Day - lent him £2, bad security."

Lane's lively interest in the world outside his own parish continued. In October 1857 there was a Day of Fast and Humiliation for the success of British soldiers in India, where the mutiny by the native sepoys had jolted complacent imperialists out of their mistaken belief in the unassailable power of the British. In his December summary of the year Lane wrote,

> *"At this period last year England was rejoicing in the prospect of a long Peace after a very disastrous war (in the Crimea), but how soon, alas, was joy turned into sorrow, in the month of June, one of the most horrid mutinies ever recorded in the history of mankind, took place in our East Indian possessions, the Sepoy troops rebelled against their officers and simultaneously throughout a vast portion of that extensive region butchered them down in cold blood, sparing neither men, women or children their object was entirely to extirpate every European to be found the cruel mutilations of defenceless women and children will never be forgot."*

A more cautious attitude needed to be - and eventually was - adopted by the British to their colonies but Lane summed up the sense of outrage felt by people all over England when he went on,

> *"but I hope that a retributive justice will speedily overtake the perpetrators of those horrid deeds. We have now upwards of 20,000 English troops in India, and they have been for the last 3 months serving them out to the amount of scores of thousands."*

By December 1858 Lane was relieved that the violence in India was now "almost extinguished" and optimistic that trade with "those hitherto almost unknown countries", China and Japan, was likely to be beneficial to England. Unfortunately, Britain had not yet learned much from its activities in India about sensitivity to foreign cultures, and other eastern countries understandably sought to resist its empire building.

But there were peaceful developments, too, such as the Atlantic Telegraph and the national railway network, on which Lane remarked. It was also a time of growing interest in geology: Lane's reference in 1858 to geologists at the Gullet predates the commercial exploitation of that quarry at the southern end of the Malvern Hills, where recent work has highlighted the different strata deposited in the upheavals which threw up the hills millions of years ago.

In March 1859 he was summoned, with 14 others from Castlemorton, for jury service at Worcester Assizes, and spent hours waiting about, his record showing that not much has changed for jurors since 1859.

> *"In court by 9 and stayed till near 7, not on the jury, only 3 trials, viz. 1 rape, 1 exposing person and 1 receiving silver plate knowing it to be stolen."*

When discharged on the third day he wrote "Mem: Never served on a petty jury nor now never will." It was one of the few civic duties he did not experience.

Chapter Six 1864 - 1871
Human Frailties

The diary which Lane started in 1864 covers more years than any of the earlier ones, though contains rather less detail on farming matters, market prices and work. Now a well established elder statesman of the parish, presumably he had lost interest in the cut and thrust of trade and business during his final years. His stock seems to have decreased: when he made a report to the Board of Trade in March 1866 he declared it as 42 Cattle, 8 sheep and 8 pigs - a sizeable herd of cattle but a much reduced number of sheep from former years when he had to hire 5 shearers and sold large weights of wool. He was certainly very anxious when the dreaded rinderpest or "cattle plague" appeared in June 1865. In England 6000 animals died in a few months, the transport of cattle was prohibited and "we pray God to preserve and protect our herds." A large congregation attended church in March 1866 for a special service on "a day of humiliation on account of cattle plague." Restrictions on the movement of cattle were in effect for two years.

Considerable quantities of cider and perry were produced on his farms. In 1866 he claimed to have made 53 hogsheads of drink, which is about 2650 gallons. But some of his plans did not work out: threshing an old wheat rick in January 1867 revealed that two-thirds of it had been eaten by mice: "I make this memo. Keep no more old wheat till mice are exterminated."

In today's climate of criticism of modern farming methods we sometimes romanticise farming in the so-called "good old days": it is salutary to be reminded that farming has always been a hard and sometimes a dangerous occupation. In February 1869 Lane, using an engine, "thrashed an old bean rick...the engine burst providentially no accident." Only a month earlier he wrote "Poor Jos. Witcomb killed with hay knife" but the circumstances of this are not clear.

In May 1868 he had recorded a fatality due to a quarrel between his men, rather than actual farming practice:

> *"the most melancholy accident that has happened since my residence at Cutlers...Chas, Gunnell my cowman had geered a horse to litter the shed. This so exasperated Jones that after a few words he struck the horse with a besom, thinking to knock Gunnell down, who in return pushed Jones into the misken hole about 4 feet deep and about 2 feet of soft litter and grass, he falling on his head dislocated the 6th vertebrae of his back bone and caused his death at 10 o'clock the next morning."*

In the absence of effective trade unions employers had great power over their workers in both town and country. Hours were long and conditions hard, yet the law occasionally seems to have been on the side of the oppressed employee: Lane recorded that a local farmer was sent to prison for 21 days for thrashing a boy in 1866.

In October 1864 he referred to the "final wind-up of Upton Inclosure" but continued for two more years to record minor items connected with it, such as "sorting and arranging Upton Inclosure Papers" and drawing out £300, the surplus at the end of the proceedings, which was "distributed amongst the Freeholders" in the spring of 1866. The Drainage of Longdon Marsh was to be the next interminable saga: he attended "a great many meetings" which he clearly thought a waste of time and failed to record in any useful detail.

Some valuation work continued. In July 1864 he was at "Cowley Park" and two months later he valued Upton in order that the poor rate might be assessed. But he seems to have had less work and to have caught up with some of the jobs which had piled up in busier times, like stitching together old magazines and the newspapers of which he was clearly an avid reader. An astonishing delay is implied in an entry for September 1865 which reads: "Kendrick began rickyard wall. Stone halled in 1844." This was not the end of that particular story because Lane complained after Earl Somers' next audit, "I have laid out £30 in building shed, 2 pigs cots and Rickyard wall and now they refuse to allow it." He seems to have lost his earlier influence over his powerful Eastnor landlord but did not give up the struggle: a year later he was actually allowed half of his outlay.

In June 1866 Mrs Lane went to stay with their son John in Clerkenleap and experienced a terrifying thunder storm.

> *"The electric fluid struck the 3 front windows and smashed large panes of glass. My wife and Miss Hawkins in dining room a narrow escape."*

Preoccupied with his own health - frequent colds and pain in his legs are recorded - he made his will in March 1865. But he still kept his finger on the pulse of parochial life and continued on the board of guardians for Upton workhouse until March 1866, even though he found the behaviour of some of his fellow guardians unacceptable: in 1865 he had "had enough - dictator R. Lord rampant."

His opinions remained as strong as ever and he retained the knack of readily finding a telling phrase for anything of which he disapproved. When 4 friends came to shoot on his land he observed "4 guns. I wonder whether a single certificate" but was not officious enough openly to challenge them. In 1866 an acquaintance

> "was unfortunately kill'd by a fall from his Horse when hunting on the 2nd Feb. Aged 34 leaving a widow and 5 children. Poor fellow: I much fear that his worldly propensities overbalanced his principles of honesty and integrity."

By the end of 1864, when a Waywardens Bill was about to go through parliament, he thought "it will be an improvement on the self-serving system of parochial surveyors" - a stab at men he thought wasted money on those roads which the parish had to maintain. Some main roads were by now built and maintained by turnpike trusts, but the tolls they charged users were much resented and in 1866 Lane reported widespread agitation for the abolition of turnpikes.

He continued to give his opinion on international affairs, as at the end of 1864 in reference to the American Civil War:

> "it is expected that a reduction in the Army will take place as it has in most European nations - the Americans still keep butchering away but it is supposed that their war will soon end as the Northerners seem lately to be much in the assendant."

and in 1865,

> "In the spring the American President Lincoln was murdered and the war was ended and Slavery abolished I hope for ever."

When the 1867 Parliamentary Reform Act gave the vote to some working-class men - Lord Derby called it "a leap in the dark" - Lane expressed concern that "too much of the democratic element will overbalance the house of commons." He believed "a little war with the black King of Abyssinia in Africa" would prove expensive. His 1867 comments on Anglo-Irish politics are a depressing reminder of how long these two nations have sought to thrash out their differences:

> "The Fenian Brotherhood has lately been committing crimes of the blackest and most diabolical description as witness the shooting of Policemen, the blowing up of the Clerkenwell detention house and thereby killing of 40 or 50 innocent persons...consequently scores of thousands of 'specials' are sworn in throughout the towns of England. There have been several hanged."

In December 1868 he wrote,

> "Mr Disraeli in November dissolved the Parliament and tried the experiment of a general election on the principles of the new Reform Bill. The consequence was rioting in very many places through England, Wales and Ireland similar to those of 1832... Thank God we are at peace with all the world and long may we continue so."

He was never more blunt than in expressing his opinion of the church and clergy and, as a Castlemorton churchwarden from 1852, his opinions carried some weight. This was a controversial period in the church's history. The Oxford movement had fostered a revival of reverence in the Church of England but many people, accustomed to simple services taken by a parson in black clerical garb, perceived practices like clergy being called priests and wearing vestments as "Romish", and found them offensive. John Rayer Lane was one of them.

CASTLEMORTON CHURCH

His diary is peppered with angry and contemptuous references to the "Jesuitical priest", Rev. A. Wood, who became curate in 1865 and soon "very foolishly preached about pagan ornaments." Although he continued for some years to visit and even dine with the Lanes, he clearly blotted his copybook very quickly. He called on Lane with a request as early as August 1865, "his present want a stove in Church." This might seem a good idea to anyone who has endured a service in an unheated church in the middle of winter, but Lane was made of sterner stuff. By December he grumbled,

> "Sunday at Church enclosed Porch, Painted Door - new Fire stove and a rum sermon. What road is Castlemorton going?"

and

> "In our Protestant Church I fear greatly that Ritualism is gaining ground rapidly as the newspapers of the last week are full of descriptions of Church decorations and other tomfoolery leading to Romanism."

In February 1867 Lane was told of plans for the restoration of Castlemorton Church: "£1095 a poor prospect" was his laconic observation. He did not bother to comment on Wood's desire for a gallery in the church for the singers.

In June 1867 Lane attended the Archdeacon's visitation at Worcester and gleefully recorded the "very excellent charge to Churchwardens to do their duty and not to suffer the Clergy to decorate or bring any new fangles into the Church." For months after this he made a note of each time he went to Church and found it "decorated." He refused to lend Wood the churchwarden's book and when, as a result, "Rev. A. Wood sent me a very long and foolish letter" he "sent him a spirited answer." At the end of 1868, in his annual reflections on the past year he commented,

> "Our ecclesiastical and religious views I am sorry to say does not improve, the sensational element has got a strong hold....Jesuitical Ministers preaching and trying in many other ways to unprotestantise the Church of our Land therefore I would advize all true Christians to instruct the young in principles of the established Church of England."

This work does indeed seem to have been attempted. National Schools supporting the Church of England had been built in many towns and villages, and Lane himself refers to the consecration of two new local churches: at Hollybush in September 1869 and the Hook in 1870. Nearby Welland (1875), Hanley Swan (1873) and Upton (1879) provide further evidence of the extensive church building which took place in the latter years of the 19th century in an attempt to make the Church of England more accessible to all.

In March 1868 Lane wrote "our *priest* offended because I bespoke a *Protestant* surplice off J. Farr (the Upton tailor)." When the surplice arrived the parson, who had "got huffed but not at me" at a churchwardens' meeting, "sent me a most intemperate and offensive letter about the surplice not being lawn but mixed with cotton." In June 1868 "Priest Wood had candles lighted for evening service." On Christmas Day 1868

> *"the Priest Wood before his sermon told the congregation what he called a great secret viz. that he had obtained of Earl Somers upwards of twenty years rent charge at 10 shillings a year and a great deal of small talk out of the pulpit ..... I wish his modesty was as conspicuous as his ignorance and impudence - the parishioners of Castlemorton would estimate his character at a far higher value than at present."*

Christian charity clearly did not prevail even on this most special day in the church's calendar, and Lane did not go to Church for over five months. Mrs. Lane, however, reported developments to him: Wood had given notice on 1st May 1869 that he was going to "pull down 2 chancel seats" and she found on 2nd May that he had already "stript the chancel. What can be done to him." Lane went to church at last on 30th May to find for himself that "Priest Wood has removed the pews in chancel etc." Later, when Lane went to the church with Creese, the glazier, who was working on the chancel window, he "saw Priest Wood who like a pig grunted."

He was sad at the death of Rev. C.F. Secretan at the early age of 47 and "much respected" in Longdon and Castlemorton. Occasionally, when visiting his son John at Clerkenleap, he would go to Kempsey Church where he approved of the "very excellent clergymen." It was all in such contrast to what he had to endure at home. But there were clearly two sides: in March 1869,

> *"the Priest Wood has been perswading the Labourers of this parish that he can obtain a great quantity of land from Lord Somers for allotments for them. In consequence I heard that upwards of 70 met at the Robin Hood..., the chief object to abuse the Paymasters."*

THE ROBIN HOOD. CASTLEMORTON

If the labourers had kept diaries we might well see a viewpoint very different from Lane's, but numerous entries indicate that parish officials were concerned that Wood was trying to get power over the parish lands from which rents had traditionally been used to relieve the poor. Lane vigorously opposed this, putting steel into the parish overseers' resolve not to be outsmarted by *"Priest Wood the Dodger"*. "Time up" wrote Lane in triumph on 18th August 1869. The next week he

> *"attended the largest Parish Meeting I ever saw. Upwards of 50 persons there to consult about a scheme propounded by Wood the Curate to elect 9 trustees to manage the Church and Parish lands so that the money may come into his hands. The whole parish against him, except Joe Pope."*

Nevertheless, some change occurred because the first meeting of the Castlemorton trustees took place in March 1870 and notice to quit was sent to all occupiers of church and parish property.

In the middle of all this, in December 1868, a new vicar arrived but was scarcely more acceptable to Lane.

> *"Rev. Mr. Lefroy called on me first time and his Jesuitical Curate Wood. They want me to sign a petition to the Charity Commissioners to give up all the Lands belonging to this Parish to the Parson to give away to the Poor. Will see them D-- first."*

He declined Lefroy's dinner invitations and on the day of the trustees meeting in March 1870

> "dressed him for his troublesome officiousness ever since he became vicar ...December 1868. He wanted me to furnish him with information. I refused."

The diary entries give a vivid if disjointed picture of an unhappy state of affairs. In June 1870 Wood, from the pulpit, told Alfred Lane not to grin at him and at the afternoon service "took Jem Wadley's hat and ran out of the Church to Pope's" - the home of his loyal ally. In August he preached a sermon on the Real Presence, a belief in the effects of consecration on bread and wine in the Communion service that would have offended Lane because of its high church tendency. Others in the congregation - if they understood this arcane subject - are also unlikely to have been best pleased.

Lane had an enjoyable 5 day trip to London with his son William in October 1868, taking the train from Upton to see Mr. Wedgwood for whom he had long collected rents. They took the latest rents with them, had lunch with Mr. Wedgwood and his family, and saw "the Picture of the *eminent* Jos. Wedgwood" - Lane loved this kind of connection with fame, tenuous though it was. An excursion to the Crystal Palace on its new site at Sydenham must have brought back memories of that exciting trip of 1851. This and various other London landmarks were all "pleasant but nothing like home."

Family life was important: his mother died in 1863 (though the relevant diary is missing), his daughter Ann lived at home and the sons often visited. There were occasional summer picnics at Peter Pocket's - the predecessor of the Malvern Hills Hotel at the foot of the Herefordshire Beacon. He seems to have been aware of his children's faults: William was regularly noted as being "so-so", meaning slightly the worse for drink, and in December 1870 William and his wife spent the evening, "he as usual am sorry to say about half drunk." John, with a tendency to drive his horse-drawn vehicles too fast, had an accident on his way home to Clerkenleap in September 1869 - "No more stopping late at Cutlers." Such laconic observations were made of himself as well as others and he recognised occasionally that he himself made mistakes, like buying the works of Shakespeare in 3 volumes from a travelling salesman - "I fear I shall be done" - or lending Mrs. Stephens £14 - "a very foolish act."

In view of the detail given by Lane of many aspects of local and national life, certain omissions are strange, perhaps pointing to difficulty in articulating affection. William's wife was Harriet and John's was probably Sally but why did he so rarely refer to his grandchildren and daughters-in-law by name? They are usually mentioned as "John's wife and daughter" or "William's Children", though "Willy's 6th birthday" was noted in March 1867. In contrast, favourite horses had names, like "my poor old horse Boxer....and old Jolly his companion" for whom a grave was dug when they were so old that they had to be destroyed.

Lane had probably become rather a difficult old man. Used for years to telling others what to do, he no longer had so much professional work to keep him busy or so much influence. His mind was still very active but he was beginning to be quite seriously troubled by poor health. Along with his opinions on local and national affairs and the interminable quarrel with the local clergy he recorded his various colds, aches and minor accidents with increasing regularity and a touching faith in doctors - "he called and told me I was better." But, apart from the occasional application of leeches, his doctors - Dr Marsh and his son, Henry - gave remarkably acceptable advice: in September 1869 Lane felt very giddy and "H. Marsh recommended Champaigne. Had a bottle on trial and weak brandy water." It obviously went down well: a year later delivery of a dozen bottles is noted. In March 1870 Lane was "very unwell" and Dr. Marsh "ordered me to keep on drinking Brandy." Hopefully this was not the cause of a fall in November 1870: "in going upstairs negligently, fell down backwards 8 or 9 stairs and hurt my back very severely but not a bruise or scratch on any other part."

But maybe this mishap was the beginning of the end for John Rayer Lane. There is no surviving diary for the last few months of his life, the last entry apparently being in early 1871. He died, aged 73, in July 1871, leaving behind the wife whom he might have expected to outlive. She in fact lived another 16 years, past her 100th birthday, and died in April 1887.

Epilogue

The children and grandchildren of Elizabeth and John Rayer Lane continued to farm in the area. In 1908 Cutlers Farm - the farmhouse modernised and much enlarged from the modest home so dear to John Rayer Lane - was sold by the Eastnor estate to Worcestershire County Council, which had embarked on a somewhat controversial policy of letting out smallholdings.

Cutlers Farm, further modernised, is still tenanted and run as a working farm in the parish whose landscape still bears so much evidence of medieval Malvern Chase.

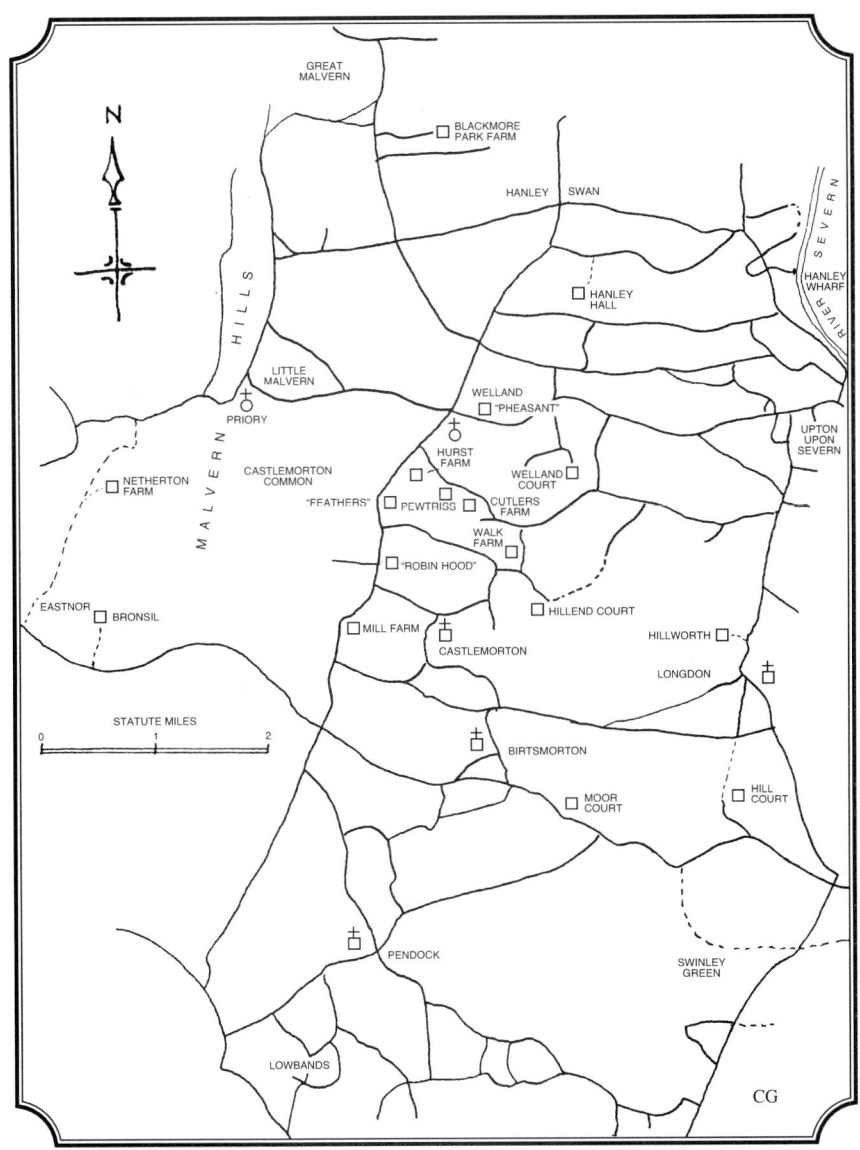